HAUNTED BOWDOIN COLLEGE

D1056493

DAVID R. FRANCIS

Haunted America

Published by Haunted America
A Division of The History Press
Charleston, SC 29403
www.historypress.net

Front cover: Hubbard Hall. *Author's collection.*
Back cover, lower: Bowdoin Chapel. *Author's collection.*

First published 2014

Manufactured in the United States

ISBN 978.1.62619.610.0

Library of Congress CIP data applied for.

CONTENTS

CONTENTS

FOREWORD

Just up the hill from the busy downtown shops, coffeehouses, restaurants and lively galleries along Maine Street, a small college quietly goes about its business in Brunswick, Maine. This small New England town with a population of around twenty thousand is nestled alongside the Androscoggin River. Tucked away in the remnants of a great pine forest at the top of the hill, Bowdoin College is a highly regarded private liberal arts school widely known for professors who are passionate about teaching and students who bring to life the college's commitment to the common good. Founded over two hundred years ago, Bowdoin College has a long history—not all of it haunted.

In 1794, Governor Samuel Adams of Massachusetts signed the charter that brought Bowdoin College into existence. Named in honor of James Bowdoin, a prominent leader of anti-British colonial activity and later governor of Massachusetts, Bowdoin College has grown from a school with seven graduates in 1806 to a student body of just under two thousand individuals today. In the years between, Bowdoin has produced a list of prestigious alumni that belies its small size. From writers and Civil War generals to politicians and Olympic gold medalists, the students who have weathered mid-coast Maine's long winters and passed through Bowdoin's halls have gone on to great achievements. Distinguished literary alumni include Henry Wadsworth Longfellow (1825) and Nathaniel Hawthorne (1825), for whom the largest library on campus is named. Joshua Lawrence Chamberlain (1852) led the Twentieth Maine at Gettysburg during the Civil

War and would later serve as governor of Maine and president of his alma mater. And from one of Bowdoin's earliest classes to admit women, alumna Joan Benoit Samuelson (1979) earned a gold medal in the first-ever women's Olympic marathon in 1984. This is but a small sampling of the college's illustrious list of alumni that also includes several U.S. senators, Supreme Court justices and a U.S. president.

A Bowdoin alumna myself, I can personally speak to the unique qualities of the institution that lead to the Bowdoin experience. Academically, Bowdoin challenged me from the start of my first year, and I can remember long, late-night conversations with my two roommates in Coleman Hall about engaging topics from my introductory sociology class. In the arena of athletics, I was on the rugby pitch with Bowdoin women from all over the country. Recreationally, I was spending time with Bowdoin's Outing Club and exploring the Atlantic coast via sea kayak. By the end of the spring, the many eye-opening experiences of my first year coalesced into a great enthusiasm for the college. As an admissions campus tour guide during my four years, I had the opportunity to share this enthusiasm with prospective students and their families, hoping to convey in one hour all that Bowdoin offered.

My rewarding student experience at Bowdoin led me to pursue a career in higher education administration, and in my first job after graduating, in the Office of Residential Life at Bowdoin, I met David Francis, who was a fellow tour guide (though I did not know that at the time). As a colleague, David was invaluable; he was the IT architect behind many of the systems that we relied on to do our work in residential life. A man who is quick to smile and has a sharp sense of humor, he was never dull to work with.

It was through Lisa Rendall, a colleague in my office, that I first heard about David's Haunted Tour. Informally, David had invited a small number of us to join him one evening after work to explore the spookier side of campus. It was late October in Maine, where the sun sets before six o'clock, when the tour group gathered in the fading daylight. Everyone was bundled up in warm coats as we roamed the quad, and David shared with us the mysterious history of campus buildings. Adams Hall stands out for me (as it probably does for most people) as the most memorable stop on the Haunted Tour. He took us down into the creepy basement, where the cadavers awaiting dissection had been stored when the medical college was located there. He directed our attention to the top of the building's staircase so we could see the hook that was used to hoist the cadavers to the top floor for dissection. I had been in Adams Hall many times as a student and must admit I was shocked to think how I passed that spot for years without thinking twice about the hook jutting out of the ceiling.

The conclusion of the tour was at Anna's grave. Throughout the tour, David had been alluding to a grave on campus. I was understandably skeptical, as I had spent a great deal of time on campus and felt that if such a thing existed, I would have noticed it. But outside one of the red brick first-year residence halls, he brought to my attention a light gray square inscribed with the name Anna. With his typical flair and encouragement for participation, he asked for guesses of what was buried at this spot. After the incorrect guesses of a student and a beloved pet, we were treated to the full story, which I won't spoil for you, but I assure you it is revealed in one of the later chapters.

The darkness of night had settled as we parted ways at the end of the tour, and I was left thinking about all the secrets of the Bowdoin College campus. I had been a tour guide, lived on campus for years and thought I knew it well, but in this one evening, I had learned many stories new to me—stories I might never have known otherwise. Knowing firsthand how these stories can enrich one's appreciation for the college, it came as no surprise to me that the enthusiasm for Haunted Bowdoin tours has continued to grow over the years and that David's collection of historical and personal accounts of the spookier side of campus has multiplied.

I can think of no better guide for a Haunted Bowdoin tour. David's enthusiasm for Halloween and spooky stories is reflected in his annual tradition of decorating his home. Each October, his home always draws attention for being the best decorated on the street. There are spider webs in the windows and alarming motion-activated devices to scare passersby. So while not all of us are fortunate enough to join one of David's tours on a chilly October evening, I am thrilled he has created this work as a resource to those who like to brush aside spider webs and hunt for the spookier history that is lurking on Bowdoin's campus.

Erica Ostermann, '06
Assistant Dean
Cornell University
Ithaca, New York

ACKNOWLEDGEMENTS

I would like to thank the George J. Mitchell Department of Special Collections and Archives for its assistance and use of its photos and material. I would also like to thank Mark Nelsen, who provided my initial threads and filled in a lot of missing pieces. I would also like to thank Ned Osolin for taking me to places on the Bowdoin campus that few people ever get to see. Thanks also to Holly Sherburne for providing the photography.

Lastly, I would like to thank all the Bowdoin students and alumni who have taken my Haunted Bowdoin tour. I have always marveled at how polite you have been and how appreciative you have seemed.

Introduction

*All houses wherein men have lived and died
Are haunted houses. Through the open doors
The harmless phantoms on their errands glide,
With feet that make no sound upon the floors.*

*We meet them at the doorway, on the stair,
Along the passages they come and go,
Impalpable impressions on the air,
A sense of something moving to and fro.*

*There are more guests at table, than the hosts
Invited; the illuminated hall
Is thronged with quiet, inoffensive ghosts,
As silent as the pictures on the wall.*

*The stranger at my fireside cannot see
The forms I see, nor hear the sounds I hear;
He but perceives what is; while unto me
All that has been is visible and clear.*

*We have no title-deeds to house or lands;
Owners and occupants of earlier dates
From graves forgotten stretch their dusty hands,
And hold in mortmain still their old estates.*

The spirit-world around this world of sense
Floats like an atmosphere, and everywhere
Wafts through these earthly mists and vapors dense
A vital breath of more ethereal air.

Our little lives are kept in equipoise
By opposite attractions and desires;
The struggle of the instinct that enjoys,
And the more noble instinct that aspires.

These perturbations, this perpetual jar
Of earthly wants and aspirations high,
Come from the influence of an unseen star,
An undiscovered planet in our sky.

And as the moon from some dark gate of cloud
Throws o'er the sea a floating bridge of light,
Across whose trembling planks our fancies crowd
Into the realm of mystery and night,—

So from the world of spirits there descends
A bridge of light, connecting it with this,
O'er whose unsteady floor, that sways and bends,
Wander our thoughts above the dark abyss.

Henry Wadsworth Longfellow wrote "Haunted Houses" for his 1847 collection of poetry *Birds of Passage*. In many ways, this poem by one of Bowdoin College's most illustrious of alumni echoes the themes I wish to pursue in this work. While always maintaining a tone of the supernatural and evoking images of spirituality, the true subject of the poem is grounded in the real memories and tangible reminders of our predecessors. For Longfellow, the past, with its endless train of but partially remembered characters and events, is all one great ghost story. Distant memories are akin to spectral whispers. Past lives surround us like intangible spirits beyond our comprehension. Following in Longfellow's path, I will present the reader with tales of spirits classically paranormal, as well as stories of unique spirits from the all-but-forgotten long ago whose essences still pervade our lives today. The result, I believe, is an olio of stories: some supernatural and others just bizarre. Some stories are more mythical and others more historical. Some are distinctly eerie, while others are simply amusing.

The origins for this work began in 2005. I had been working at Bowdoin for about four years, and as I did most days at that time, I was eating lunch with a number of longtime employees when, as autumn was setting in and Halloween approaching, we started talking about ghosts and ghost stories. When I asked some of these Bowdoin veterans if the college had any of its own ghost stories, they thought for a while but couldn't come up with any particulars. They gave me the names of a few people I should contact who knew more about Bowdoin's history, but they couldn't provide much else. I remembered I was surprised about this deficiency in stories. I felt a college that had resided in the rural outskirts of New England for over two hundred years must have developed *some* sort of reputation for the supernatural! I jotted down the names my co-workers suggested, sent a few e-mails off that afternoon to these potential sources and waited for the replies.

Sadly, this initial salvo produced little content, and what information I did get back came in very slowly. Most of the contacts were forced to admit they had very little to offer me in the way of ghost stories. A few offered the names of some retired faculty, but when I contacted these gentlemen, they had as little to offer as their referrers. A few people had suggested I look deeper into the old medical school building (Adams Hall) as it at least still had some artifacts from its days of housing cadavers and performing autopsies, so with this one slender thread, I headed to the library to do some serious research. I pored through old volumes searching for connections that might take me from the mundanely grisly to the supernatural, but I wasn't getting much in the way of actual ghost stories. On the other hand, I was certainly getting rewarded with every other kind of strange and interesting tale. Bowdoin wasn't giving up its secret ghost stories easily, but I found I was so enthralled with the history and characters of Bowdoin's past that I was content to just become a bit of an expert in this unique area of antiquity.

Then, while searching through some fairly recent newspaper articles about Adams Hall, I found a reference to the book *Ghosts of the Northeast* by David Pitkin. I hunted down the book and discovered that Pitkin had interviewed a Bowdoin College security officer and gotten a number of stories from her.

The floodgates were about to open. It turns out that I had been asking the wrong people. If you want to learn about ghost stories, you need to talk to the people who have the job of walking around in those old buildings at night when no one else is around. I immediately focused my attention on these security officers and the late-night custodial staff, and the stories started coming in. They, in turn, were able to direct me to even more people, and soon I was moving from the occasional story of unexplained incidents in the dead of night to bits of legend and folklore among the faculty and students.

I had collected a fair number of stories by the middle of October, and evenings on the campus were taking on the Halloween-like aura that only New England can provide. While strolling back through campus on my way home on one of these evenings, I saw an admissions tour moving along the campus quadrangle. It occurred to me then that some of my friends might enjoy hearing some of these stories I had gathered, and what better way to relay them than in a walking tour at night? So a few weeks before Halloween, I organized my jumble of notes into a collection of cue cards and sent out a handful of electronic invitations to the very first Haunted Bowdoin tour. I wanted to describe in the invitation just what people should expect, for I was quite worried about "overselling" the event. No one, I knew, was going to be "wracked with terror" by the contents of my tour, but I hoped that the stories would pique an interest in my friends as they had in me. Still, there was a voice in the back of my head that reminded me that I had always had an affinity for historical minutiae and odd trivia and that there was a strong possibility that I was going to bore my friends. So I played down subject matter as much as I could, and the invitations promised simply "a tour around the campus to some areas that have interesting, humorous, and even disturbing connections to Halloween."

Even with this modest description, the response to the invitations was immediate and enthusiastic. Every person I invited jumped at the opportunity, and the ranks of the group swelled as many of the invitees asked to bring members of their families along. Even with this response, I was still apprehensive about how the actual tour would be received. I remember one friend asked if she could bring her daughter or whether the tour would be too scary.

"How old is she?" I asked.

"Twelve," she replied.

"Oh, I think there is a greater chance she will be bored than scared," I sighed.

Well, my friends all went, and that twelve-year-old went too, and none of them seemed in the least bit bored. The success of that inaugural tour was a great surprise and pleasant relief to me. A few weeks later, I received an e-mail from a student who had heard about my tour and wanted to take her college house members on it. Immediately, all my worries returned.

It was one thing to think I could entertain my friends who knew me and shared some of my interests, but it was something else entirely to imagine I could interest a group of twenty-year-olds who might have little or no appreciation for my odd little collection of tales. I recall that I cautioned the student along these very lines, but she dismissed my concerns so confidently that I felt I had to make the attempt. As darkness fell while I sat at our agreed-on meeting spot to start the tour, I remember telling myself, "If this goes awfully and the students look miserable, just wrap it up quickly and let them get back to their studies."

But it wasn't awful. The students seemed truly interested in all my stories and were incredibly polite. I felt they put as much into enjoying the experience as I did and had amped themselves up enough that by the time we gathered in the basement of Adams Hall to discuss the unsettling things that had gone on down there, the students were anxiously holding hands and looking around fearfully. At the end of the tour, the students all applauded and thanked me over and over. I remember walking back home thinking I might have found something people genuinely enjoyed.

After these successes, news of the tour spread by word of mouth. More co-workers heard about it and insisted I set up an event for them. Students heard rumors about a guy in IT who had spotted ghosts on campus, and they began to reach out to me as well. Soon I was giving several tours a year. Eventually, the college even took an interest in a semi-official manner, and I was commissioned to lead staff retreats, visiting officials and potential students on the Haunted Bowdoin tour.

As the popularity of the tour grew, I started to collect more and more stories. By the time I was first enlisted by Bowdoin's Department of Alumni Relations to provide a number of my Haunted Bowdoin tours for its summer reunion event in 2012, I had more stories at my disposal than I could really use on a tour. The reunion event coordinator asked me how much time I usually needed for my tour. I responded that a typical tour could be anywhere from thirty minutes to about three hours in length.

"Three hours!" she gasped. "Just how haunted *is* this place?"

I quickly reassured her that what she was probably looking for in a tour would be about forty-five minutes in length. In that time I would be able to cover most of the spooky, mysterious and ghastly events and places on campus. However, I cautioned, with only the slightest bit of encouragement from an engaged and inquisitive audience, I was perfectly capable of extending the tour for hours, regaling an audience with all the odd bits of trivia I have gathered in my research. For every report of an apparition in a building, there are one hundred interesting stories that are tangentially connected and provide a deeper insight into the location we are visiting. And I find the kind of audiences that are interested in haunted happenings are often equally interested in tales that don't strictly fall under the auspices of the supernatural but are equally as off-beat and little-known. When I find myself with that sort of audience, the tour can go on and on.

And so the length of a tour really depends on the degree to which I indulge myself in relating these various details. For the purposes of this book, I will admit I have indulged myself *thoroughly*. This creation is entitled *Haunted Bowdoin College,* and the reader may be sure that we will cover many stories and rumors of the paranormal. At the same time, we will visit stories and characters that have the distinction of being only rather odd or just simply amusing. The ardent ghost hunter may have to pick through certain chapters to get directly to his or her needs. On the other hand, the lover of folklore and local history and Bowdoin enthusiasts should find each chapter engaging.

If readers of this book enjoy these stories as much as I have enjoyed conveying them to my various audiences over the years, then I will consider this a great success. And if I should in return receive even more tales as a response to this publication, I will be so much the happier. When it comes to adding ghost stories, I don't usually concern myself with the facts of the story nearly as much as I do the earnestness of the source. For example, if the staff members of the college infirmary report that they have experienced myriad unexplained phenomena and choose to ascribe those events to the ghost of young Dudley Coe despite the fact that young Dudley died years before the building was constructed, I feel that only adds an extra sense of mystery to the story (if not Dudley, then what?). Along those lines, I should perhaps conclude this introduction the way I have concluded all my live tours from the very start. I provide my audience with a brief explanation of how I vet the stories I hear and choose to incorporate them. As long as the relator of the tale seems sincere, then "I have a strict scientific method," I assure them. "Someone tells me 'I heard once that...' and I tell them:

'I'll use it!'"

Chapter 1

EVERYDAY GHOSTS

He but perceives what is; while unto me
All that has been is visible and clear.

The ghosts of Bowdoin College surround the visitor to the campus at almost every turn. The young student crossing the quadrangle only occasionally looking up from a mobile device to greet a friend or avoid a speeding bicycle may walk right past many such ghosts and never even realize it. A busy professor may walk by a familiar spot several times a day and never realize the area contains some old relic of forgotten times. Even a keen observer such as I fancy myself to be may still discover new artifacts, uncover unseen manuscripts or hear new tales that further reveal the long and rich history of the institution. While in the late stages of preparing this manuscript, while researching the "Anna stones" (see Chapter 17) outside Appleton Hall, I happened to stumble on a *Whispering Pines* article by Bowdoin current historian-laureate John Cross that revealed another stone I had never seen lying just outside the walkway by Massachusetts Hall. What a treat to get to campus early the next morning to scour the ground, brushing away the light dusting of snow that had fallen the previous evening until I located the object that had been fashioned by ingenious and enterprising students some one-hundred-odd years ago.

This discovery was just another example of the everyday ghosts of Bowdoin College that will show themselves to the willing observer. They can seem as disturbing and out of time as any apparition (like the "cadaver

An Anna stone from the class of 1877 set on the east side of Massachusetts Hall. *Author's collection.*

The cadaver hook in Adams Hall. One of the few holdovers from the days of the medical school that survived the 2007 renovations. *Holly Sherburne.*

hook" that hangs in Adams Hall) or as mysterious and intriguing as spectral whispers in an old building at night (like the cryptic etching of "CWINDS LIVES" in the foundations around Hubbard Hall). Some you might stumble into suddenly during an everyday routine, like the plaque of Treasurer Clark I blundered into while on a walk (see Chapter 17), while others require trips to hard-to-find places, like those serious ghost-hunters you see on television delving into old attics and basements in search of elusive electromagnetic field readings. I imagine there aren't many people in all of Bowdoin who can say they have opened up the trapdoor on the roof of Hubbard Hall's one-hundred-foot tower and walked out to see where the various alumni who have scaled that turret and left their markings touting the achievement (Donald MacMillan, who has a museum named after him in Hubbard Hall today, left one such relic on that roof).

Like spirits that aren't quite ready to depart this earth, these many relics connect us to Bowdoin's deep history, and encounters with them affect us in a unique and personal way that general histories do not. And happily, though many college constituents scurry by these haunts without a moment's

A mysterious message left in the foundations of Hubbard Hall. The text reads, "CWINDS LIVES." *Author's collection.*

pause, there are still those on campus who are aware of these artifacts and their import. How appropriate it was that while I was crawling around on the ground outside Massachusetts Hall during my search for an Anna stone that I should be spotted by Ned Osolin as he was walking across campus on some errand. Ned has worked in the telecommunications area of Bowdoin for many years, and his work troubleshooting the phone systems on campus has led him into just about every nook and cranny of every building. Ned introduced me to many of the stories covered in this book, and without him, I wouldn't have been able to research or photograph them. Ned had never seen this particular relic either, but he reminded me that over on Winthrop Hall, just one building over, more mementos of the past were stamped on the north-facing wall of that dormitory. They are easy to miss, and the building looks like the other three brick dormitories on the quadrangle. However, get within ten feet of the entrance, and you realize the wall is a great collection of inconspicuous graffiti stretching from the archway of the entrance all around the north side and trickling off a few feet onward on the west wall. For hundreds of years, students have been engraving their initials and class years on that wall. Winthrop Hall was erected in 1822, so when a student leaves his name and class year as '33, it isn't always clear if that is 1833 or 1933, but that only serves to add more mystery to the scene. In another twenty years, people will try to decide if the class year was 1833, 1933 or 2033. Those future generations as well as our own will have reason to thank Ned, for he had a hand in preserving these artifacts by reminding the crew that had come to do repair work on the building a few years back to be careful not to mar these etchings.

Above, left: An engraving preserved on the north wall of Winthrop Hall from when the building was only nine years old (1831). *Author's collection.*

Above, right: A masonic symbol with the date 1861 carved into the foundations of the chapel by person or persons unknown. *Author's collection.*

Opposite: The heavily marked and carved inner door in the chapel. The unknown "FLAGPOLE IKE" left this message after participating in the "Great Revolution." *Author's collection.*

On the inner doors of the nearby chapel, there exists a similar collection of signatures carved or written into the old wood. One of the markings connects us to the events of the "Great Revolution" (see Chapter 6), but surely each one has a story behind it. One can spend a good hour scanning that door, noting odd symbols, surprising dates and suggestive initials. Some, like "FLAGPOLE IKE," we might be able to form connections from and link to other historic events, while others remain a mystery whose meaning could only be clear to the anonymous author. On just the opposite side of the chapel, there remains etched in a foundation wall of the basement an artifact apparently left in 1861. The letters before the year may be a date (September 12?), but there is no mistaking the square and compass symbol of Freemasonry. Who left this symbol for us and why? Was someone working on the building a secret Free Mason and saw an opportunity to tout his association when no one else was looking? We can only speculate.

A historian would like to have everything preserved and unchanged (as nonsensical as a study of history would be if that were ever to happen), and Bowdoin College has certainly lost much of its past that would have been wonderful to see. What a thrill it would have been to see the great Cleaveland Cabinet in full array in the center of Massachusetts Hall or the large mural of undersea life that once greeted visitors to the Searles Science Building but has now been covered up by simple drywall and girders. I wish the old Thorndike Oak, planted on a whim in 1802, that graced the quadrangle for almost two hundred years was still standing as a living testimony to the college's origins. And I still find myself wishing Adams Hall could have been spared its 2007 renovation that forever robbed it of much of its creepy and dilapidated charm.

Still, Bowdoin College has performed an admirable balancing act between progressing and preserving and has taken care to leave us at least fragments of almost every era. In an official capacity, departments such as the George J. Mitchell Department of Special Collections and Archives have amassed and catalogued more history than one person could ever hope to review, and extensive photos of the Cleaveland Cabinet are available there with enough different perspectives that you can almost envision the display in three dimensions. The Thorndike Oak is gone, but a slice of its trunk is still on display in the Peary MacMillan Arctic Museum and Arctic Studies Center, and a new Thorndike Oak was planted in 1996 to take the place of the old icon. Adams Hall badly needed an upgrade, but the workers took care to leave the infamous "cadaver hook" in place though it has served no practical purpose for almost one hundred years now. Even more relics dot the campus that I will not iterate here for fear of straying too far from the subject at hand.

It is probably the discovery of the mere remnants of these bygone wonders that keeps us fascinated by the bigger scene we can never see. When we are forced to fill in the missing pieces with our imagination, there is no limit to the wonder we can evoke. Surely this is what drives the creation of any ghost story—either the paranormal (of which Bowdoin certainly has its fair share, as you will discover in the following chapters) or the more ordinary everyday ghosts we may encounter daily. Supernatural or mundane, a ghost story without a backstory or an imagination can only be a strange light, an odd sound or a dead object. We must be able to put ourselves in the mind frame of our ghosts if we are to understand why they left us these histories or why, in some cases, they might refuse to fade into history at all.

Chapter 2

AN APPETITE FOR FEAR

There are more guests at table, than the hosts
Invited…

Built in 1964 as part of the Coles Tower complex that looms over the southern end of the campus, you might not think this construction was old enough to have earned a reputation for the paranormal. Indeed, the students who reside in the tower report no problems, and the staff and students who file into the dining hall each day experience nothing to disturb their meals. But the basement that lies beneath the food service area has long been a source of rumor and unease among the dining staff.

The basement is inaccessible to the general public as it is dedicated almost exclusively to the behind-the-scenes tasks of the campus dining service. The far end of the basement is an area for uniform storage and lockers for staff. At the other end is a service elevator for moving supplies back and forth to the dining hall. Most of the space in between is filled with rows of shelves that tower over visitors, each one laden with utensils, pots, containers and dry goods. The basement is clean and dry but not brightly lit, and it has a stark, functional aura to it. It has been described as "a cross between a dungeon and a fallout shelter." As Mark Dickey, the unit manager for Thorne Hall says, "The place is *very* spooky when the building is empty…you can feel someone watching and a presence when you are alone in the basement."

For years, staff have complained of upsetting and perplexing incidents, and no one cares to go down to the cellar at night alone. Lights in the hallway frequently switch on and off for no apparent reason, and the elevator doors at the far end of the basement open and close of their own accord. Several employees have complained about hearing voices when working alone. One employee who was working by himself in the dish room one night reported that he heard voices whispering in the walls. The next night, after complaining about it again, he walked off in the middle of his shift and never came back.

One staff person told me the general consensus is that the spirit in the basement is female. This may stem from another incident that used to occur. At one time, the dining staff began to use an old closet in the cellar for storing condiments. They cleared out the bric-a-brac that had been in

The basement of Thorne Dining has unsettled staff for years. The elevators are at the far end. *Holly Sherburne.*

there and found among the clutter a portrait of some woman out of early Bowdoin history. Every morning for several weeks, when someone went to get condiments from that closet, they discovered the portrait had somehow found its way back inside.

So what could be the source of this paranormal activity? Prior to the construction, the area of the complex was simply an open grassy space. But when workmen were laying the foundations, they excavated many Civil War–era artifacts such as plates and utensils from the site. Is the Thorne basement dug directly into the bowels of some older dining area that history has forgotten? An examination of the relics recovered from the site might provide more answers, but they seem to have gone missing. A staff person thought Brunswick's Pejepscot Historical Society took them into possession, but the historical society has not been able to locate any record of these items in its collection. If they have, indeed, vanished again from the knowledge of the world, then the only remaining source of information we have to unravel this mystery may be the continuing interactions that the brave and reliable Bowdoin dining staff report back to us from their forced sojourns below Coles Tower.

Chapter 3

NOBLE SPIRITS

The struggle of the instinct that enjoys,
And the more noble instinct that aspires.

For the first few years I gave the Haunted Bowdoin tour, I would prepare to cross College Street on the way to the Hawthorne-Longfellow Library, and an individual from the tour group would invariably ask, "What about the Russwurm Center? Does it have any ghosts?" I would sadly report that I had never heard of any but that I was still researching it and would welcome any information anyone could give me. As I gave more tours to students and alumni, I finally started getting some feedback I could use. A number of students mentioned that when working in the building at night, they would suddenly be subjected to intense and localized drops in temperature, even on summer evenings. An alumna told me that while studying in the small library there, a shadow of an individual appeared on the far wall and passed on out of the room even though there was no one else around. A number of these same people also reported odd tapping sounds that would reverberate through the building at no particular time or season.

Curiously, not one of the people reported feeling terribly upset by these incidents, and none of them concluded their stories with a phrase I am familiar with that runs something like "and I got out of there as fast as I could!" In many ways, this isn't surprising, for if the Russwurm Center does have any spirits from the past lingering in its walls, they are almost sure to be very decent apparitions, for history tells us that the building has always been home to gentle and noble people.

The building was constructed in 1827 for Professor Alpheus Spring Packard, a graduate of Bowdoin College (1816) who dedicated his entire life to the college, serving as a faculty member for sixty-five years. He was also in his lifetime a librarian, minister, college president and archivist. The Alpheus Spring Packard Gateway stands just across the street from the house and honors the years of service he gave to the institution.

In 1836, Packard sold half of his house to William Smyth (1822), a professor of mathematics and natural sciences. The two professors and their families lived side by side for the next thirty-five years.

William Smyth was as civic-minded as his neighbor, and in addition to his work as a professor for the college, he worked to improve the quality of the public school system throughout Maine. We learn from his son's reminiscences that he was also an "ardent lover of freedom...with an intense hatred of oppression in every form." Among the causes of freedom he championed

The Russwurm African American Center, formerly the Packard-Smyth House, was possibly a stop along the Underground Railroad at one time. *Author's collection.*

William Smyth and Alpheus Spring Packard, two of the great "souls" of Bowdoin College. *From Louis C. Hatch,* The History of Bowdoin College.

were Poland's struggle for freedom from Russia and Germany, Hungary's attempt to unshackle itself from the medieval laws and customs that still governed its people and the plight of the Cherokees who were forcibly removed from their lands. He was a staunch and outspoken abolitionist, frequently writing articles and speaking at public meetings on the evils of slavery. "He was often threatened with personal violence," his son remembers. "But nothing deterred him from doing what he believed to be right."

The Packard-Smyth house became a stop on the Underground Railroad, according to George Adams Smyth. He could recall as a child seeing escaped slaves arriving at the house in the evening and being given assistance and directions to the next station as they made their desperate attempt for the safety of Canada. Runaway slaves were not the only ones facing danger. In accordance with the Fugitive Slave Law of 1850, if William Smyth had ever been caught assisting these runaways, he could have been fined $1,000 and sentenced to up to six months in prison.

William Smyth's final act of munificence was to oversee the construction of Memorial Hall on the Bowdoin campus. This building was to honor the veterans of the recently ended Civil War, especially the Bowdoin alumni who had served in its battles. Smyth not only raised $20,000 for the project, but he also took an active hand in the construction itself. George Adams Smyth tells us that it was after overexerting himself while laying out the foundation lines for Memorial Hall that he experienced an attack and was forced to stumble home. Staggering up to the bedroom on the second floor, he lay down to rest but was again seized with an attack and passed away on April 5, 1868.

If some residual spiritual energy of William Smyth has remained in the house since that day he died on the second floor almost 150 years ago, it is no surprise that people are not alarmed by the lingering presence of this noble and generous spirit. Certainly, Smyth would have no objections to the use the college has made of his old abode. In 1970, the house was rededicated as the John Brown Russwurm African American Center.

Chapter 4

BOWDOIN'S DEATHTRAP

...the illuminated hall
Is thronged with quiet, inoffensive ghosts,
As silent as the pictures on the wall.

Built in 1903 to serve as Bowdoin College's library, Hubbard Hall, with its Gothic architecture, long façade and looming one-hundred-foot-high tower, looks as though it came right from an Edgar Allan Poe story. On rainy nights when fog enshrouds the neighboring buildings and the lights from its upper halls stream blue illumination from the fifteen-foot-tall, iron-wrought windows, it is easy to imagine Hubbard Hall as a lonely mansion on a remote estate in some forgotten countryside. Helping to complete this picture, the building features a rarity in modern architecture: a fully operating gargoyle that juts out from the top of the tower's eastern side. This gargoyle is a replica of the original gargoyle consigned to the building in 1903. The original was replaced in 2007 after nearly one hundred years of weather had worn it down and caused several fissures.

Historically, gargoyles on buildings serve two purposes. Firstly, they are built to prevent water from collecting on rooftops and to convey it away from the sides of buildings. You can see Hubbard's gargoyle doing this task on just about any rainy day. But traditionally, gargoyles had a second purpose, which was to frighten away evil spirits with their terrifying appearance. Based on the stories Hubbard Hall has to offer, we might question how well

The Hubbard Hall gargoyle is a replica of the original placed on the building in 1903. *Author's collection.*

From the gargoyle's vantage point on campus for the last one hundred years, its watchful eye seems to have missed a number of unwelcome spirits. *Holly Sherburne.*

it is serving in that role, for Hubbard Hall features high on our list of spooky places on campus.

There is no getting around the fact that Hubbard Hall has been a dangerous building. Of all the buildings I have researched on campus, no other brought up as many references to untimely deaths. One wintry morning in 1973, Athern Daggett, professor of government and class of 1925, slipped on ice on the front steps and died later in the hospital (the iron rails you see adorning the stairs today were added as a result of this unfortunate accident). John C. Donovan, a government professor, had a heart attack in his office on the second floor. A payroll clerk employee suffered the same fate in her basement office and was found slumped over the IBM 1620 she was working on.

In *Ghosts of the Northeast*, Louann Dustin-Hunter, a former security officer at Bowdoin, calls Hubbard Hall "the freakiest building on campus." The number of historic portraits lining the walls of this aged edifice undoubtedly

The steps of Hubbard Hall. Note the iron railings added after the passing of Athern Daggett. *Holly Sherburne.*

sets part of that mood. On the first floor, you are greeted with a portrait of the building's chief donor and namesake, Thomas Hubbard, as well as his wife and other worthies of Bowdoin's past. Moving up the iron-railed stone staircase to the second floor, you are met with a portrait of every president in Bowdoin College's long history going back to 1802. Each portrait seems to stare down sternly on the innocent visitor, and when the moonlight washes into the landing through the high-arching iron-paned windows that span the two floors, the entire building takes on an aura of a great and forbidding mansion.

A visitor enters Hubbard Hall via two large oak doors that creak heavily on their old hinges. Stepping inside, he enters what was originally the parlor or coatroom for the college's library. As revealed in *Ghosts of the Northeast*, at this spot on a night several years ago, a security officer was securing the building and locking it up for the night. As he was standing just inside the large wooden doors and preparing to leave, he heard a voice call out, "Hello?"

Thinking he must have missed a student somewhere, he called out with a hello of his own, and when he received no reply, he walked through the building again, searching for the source of the strange voice.

He found no one. Getting ready to leave, he suddenly heard the voice again: "Hello?"

He repeated his search again, checking every room and closet, but found no signs of life. As he prepared to lock up a third time, he heard the voice again: "Hello?"

This time, the officer went ahead and locked up the building. He had decided whatever was making that call wasn't something he was going to find.

A visitor needs only move a few more feet inside up the first flight of stairs to find the location of another famous incident. This story involves a custodian working alone after midnight when the building was locked and empty. There is a long rug that runs the length of the lobby area in front of the rooms that house Bowdoin's Arctic Museum. The custodian had vacuumed and then rolled up and set this rug against a wall so he could mop the floor. He went to the basement to fill his bucket and retrieve his mop, and when he came back up, the carpet was lying out on the floor in its original location. He scratched his head and concluded that he must have absentmindedly rolled it back out before he headed downstairs, so he just rolled it up again, set it against the wall and proceeded to mop.

View of first and second floors of Hubbard Hall. Thomas Hubbard's suite of rooms was behind the wall on the right. *Author's collection.*

With the floor mopped, he decided to take a break while the floor dried. He locked up the building behind him and went for a short walk outside to meet some of his fellow custodians. When he told them about the rug incident, they confirmed that strange things like that had been known to happen in Hubbard Hall.

When he returned from his break, he found the floor dry—and the carpet once again inexplicably lying unrolled on the floor.

The custodian immediately walked to the security office, left his keys and told the dispatcher to tell his boss he had quit. He never came back.

Joyce Whittemore joined Bowdoin's housekeeping department in 1992, and one of her first assignments was the third shift in Hubbard Hall. Working alone in the dark and empty building, Joyce liked to play her radio as she cleaned rooms. She would plug her radio in on the first floor and leave it playing loudly enough that she could hear it as she worked her way up to the third floor and back down. The problem was that night after night, she would get to the third floor, and the radio would go off. She would come back down to check on it and find it had been unplugged. She *knew* no one

The first floor of Hubbard Hall. The mysterious moving runner is in the foreground. *Author's collection.*

else was in the building because she was personally going through every room to clean and straighten it up.

Whittemore is a practical-minded individual and not easily rattled, so even though she couldn't explain the radio incidences, she didn't let them bother her, but she had another recurring problem that she felt required some sort of response. At the back of the building in between the first and second floors, there is a small landing with a set of faculty offices and, even farther back, a flight of stairs that leads up to an old lavatory. She would clean the bathroom first and then go on to tidy up the offices. A number of times as she was walking back out into the landing, she would hear the sound of water running from the upstairs lavatory. She would ascend the stairs and discover that a faucet in the sink had been turned on, and water would be gushing into the basin. She knew she would never leave the water going like that, so she couldn't explain what was going on.

"It happened again, and I threw my hands up and I said, 'Enough!'" Speaking to the room and whomever or whatever was listening, she said, "I don't mind you using the sink, and I don't mind you being here, but turn the water off when you're done!"

And that was the last time Whittemore had a problem with that bathroom.

"When I first started in Hubbard, people told me stuff like that happened, but I thought 'Whatever,'" Whittemore says. "But these things did happen to me, so I don't know."

A more recent incident occurred in the early morning hours on the second floor in the Shannon Room that was getting a remodeling. Two workers were alone in the building installing new blinds for the room's large, cathedral-style windows, and the job required a number of trips back and forth to their van. The only problem was that they could not get the wooden doors to stay unlocked so they could carry their supplies in. What made this particularly interesting was that these doors required a key to lock them unless a person was inside and remained inside after locking them. Twice they went down for supplies and returned to find the room unaccountably locked. At one point, one man left the room to check on a breaker, leaving the other man behind. As he left, he made sure the door was unlocked and couldn't be closed without a key. Nevertheless, the man left in the room was interrupted from his work a few minutes later by his companion knocking on the door to get in. Once again, the door had managed to lock itself. "I might add," Ernie Hartford, one of the two men, said, "that the latch on this lock had to be turned closed with a handle, and it did not move so easily that it would just fall into a locked position by itself."

Second-floor hallway of Hubbard Hall leading to the Shannon Room. The mysterious relocking doors can be seen toward the back. *Author's collection.*

What might be the source of these activities? Well, it may be connected with the building's namesake and patron, Thomas Hubbard, of the class of 1857. After graduating from Bowdoin, Hubbard studied law, and following his service in the Union army in the Civil War, he undertook several business interests. Bowdoin College benefited considerably from his philanthropy, and the college remained close to his heart all his life. As a perk of being the donor for the building, Thomas Hubbard actually had a suite of rooms he lived in on the second floor of Hubbard Hall, across from the Bliss room. Susan Kaplan, professor of anthropology and director of the Peary-MacMillan Arctic Museum and Arctic Studies, is the current resident, the suite having been converted to office spaces following Hubbard's death in 1915. Some of the furniture from Hubbard's days remains today, and Kaplan states that for years, the doors of an old liquor cabinet in the office used to start shaking on their own when she was alone in the office.

"Some people are decidedly uncomfortable in the building, particularly at night," says Kaplan. "I have always considered Hubbard Hall's ghost, who

I assume is Thomas Hubbard, a congenial spirit, even though it does move stuff around the building and makes noise in my office on occasion. But then, I am an archaeologist, and I dig old things!"

Rather than becoming alarmed by these events, Kaplan decided to take a proactive and unique approach to quell the restless spirit. She surmised that by shaking those liquor cabinet doors, the spirit was giving her a hint, and so she made sure there was always at least one bottle of strong spirits in that cabinet. As long as the cabinet was stocked, the strange activities in her office subsided.

Professor Kaplan may have worked out an arrangement with her ethereal officemate, but others still have run-ins with this turbulent spirit. Also in this office is an old bell used in the time of Thomas Hubbard's residence to ring for servants. A custodian walking by the closed office one night reported that he heard the bell ringing away on its own. He understandably did not investigate further.

More recently, a person seems to have had an encounter with Thomas Hubbard himself. A staff person coming into the building in the very early hours of the morning saw a figure in a Civil War uniform ascending the stairs to the second-floor landing just as she was preparing to go up the stairs herself. When she got to the second floor, no one was there. The observer,

A view of Thomas Hubbard's suite. *Bowdoin College Archives, Brunswick, Maine.*

Thomas Hubbard as a colonel in the Union army. *Brady National Photographic Art Gallery, (Wikipedia).*

who has insisted on staying anonymous, says she has no particular interest in ghosts and, what is more, didn't even know that Thomas Hubbard had a distinguished career as a general in the Civil War before he had the building commissioned. What put the image of a Civil War uniform into her head if not an apparition of the general himself is hard to explain.

Do you agree with Louann Dustin-Hunter's assessment that Hubbard Hall is the "freakiest building on campus"? It certainly has provided the most varied assortment of tales. And somehow, I can't help thinking Hubbard Hall isn't finished providing us with stories quite yet!

Chapter 5

A FLY IN THE OINTMENT

A sense of something moving to and fro.

As I mentioned in the preceding chapter, traversing the hall of the second story of Hubbard Hall can be a spooky experience with the eyes of all of Bowdoin's past presidents gazing down at you from their high-mounted portraits. The portrait of recent Bowdoin College president Robert H. Edwards appears like the rest of the portraits in the landing, but take a closer look at the gentleman's right hand. Is that image of an insect an odd tattoo, a curious birthmark or some sinister artifact added by the artist for reasons unknown?

In fact, this mark was added at the request of President Edwards. During his tenure from 1990 through 2001, the same Susan Kaplan mentioned in the previous chapter who occupies Thomas Hubbard's old suite of rooms was associate dean for academic affairs and later the acting dean. Part of the job of being a dean, of course, is attending formal events held by the college, and once she started attending, Professor Kaplan felt the need to add some flavor to the president's otherwise solemn and respectful gatherings. She began bringing a pocketful of little plastic spiders or flies and would place them in various places when no one was looking. "First I planted a fly on a bar of soap in the bathroom, but then I got more ambitious," Kaplan says. For a while, the appearances of these insects at events remained a mystery to the administration, but eventually people began to catch on. She got an e-mail from President Edwards one day informing her that Cleaveland

President Edwards portrait with inset of the mysterious object on the right hand. *Author's collection.*

House (where the events were held) seemed to have an "infestation" and that he felt that as a director of a museum she would know how to stop it. But getting caught did not discourage Professor Kaplan. At one event, she remembers, the president's wife stopped her as she was entering. "I walked in, and she insisted on checking my pockets, which I let her do…[the plastic insects] were in my hand."

Kaplan kept the prank going for years, even surreptitiously attaching a plastic spider to the president's academic regalia when he was to receive an honorary degree from the college. When President Edwards stepped down from the presidency in 2001, his portrait was added to the second floor of Hubbard Hall alongside the college's other illustrious leaders. But he instructed the artist to include a fly in the portrait in fond memory of the "infestation" that plagued his term in office. It was certainly an appropriate coup de grâce to the affair, for as many times as Kaplan had managed to surprise President Edwards with the sudden appearance of one of her plastic insects, she certainly never expected to see one appear there. "It was a complete and total surprise to me to see the fly on his hand. I guess I made more of an impression in an odd way than I had thought."

Chapter 6

DEVILISH BEHAVIOR

These perturbations, this perpetual jar...

Since my Haunted Bowdoin tour is typically in highest demand around Halloween time, I often get asked to tell stories about famous pranks played through the years on the campus. There have certainly been a number of escapades by students over the years, but the one I usually settle on is the infamous "Flagpole Incident."

One Sunday morning in the spring of 1930, the campus administrators discovered a puzzling scene on the quadrangle. The doors of the college chapel were left open, and jutting several feet beyond them was one end of the seventy-five-foot flagpole that was slated to be installed in the middle of the quad. The other end of the pole was resting all the way down at the far end of the chapel right up against the lectern. Furthermore, out on the quad where the wooden staging for this potential memorial had been erected, now only smoldering embers remained.

What was the reason for this apparent wanton act of vandalism? Anarchists? Revolutionaries? Anti-American instigators?

In fact, the act of sabotage that had been inflicted on the flagpole and staging was a result of a number of students deciding to take definitive action over their objections to this memorial.

The college had been working for several years to devise a proper memorial for the Great War and the twenty-nine Bowdoin graduates who had been lost to its ravages. When the plans began to take shape, the

The Flagpole Incident, or the "Great Revolution." Note the suited administrators overseeing in the background. *Bowdoin College Archives, Brunswick, Maine.*

location picked by the architects and approved by the committee was the middle of the quad. Although the student council gave its "unanimous vote of confidence" for this location, many in the student body were offended by the choice, feeling that the quad was their own space. Most of the faculty also felt the location was a poor choice, as it would require removing trees and would split the otherwise open and bucolic expanse into two smaller, less attractive lots. Despite this opposition, the committee stuck to the original plan, and matters came to a head that Saturday night.

Removing the flagpole from where it had been deposited was difficult enough, but deciding how to proceed was even trickier. Fifty years earlier, the college had faced open insurgence from the student body in the form of the infamous 1874 "Drill Rebellion" in which three-quarters of the male students refused to participate in the mandatory military drill that President Chamberlain had established two years prior. The resulting dismissal of the better part of the student body led to a messy and protracted struggle among students, faculty and administration, and in 1930, President Sills didn't wish

Today's students seem to have made peace with the flagpole at its preferred location. *Author's collection.*

for a repeat of that experience. The Memorial Committee reconvened and by June 18 had agreed on placing the flagpole and its pedestal at its current location between Hubbard Hall and the Walker Art Museum.

Visitors to the college can still see an enduring relic of the Flagpole Incident. As mentioned in Chapter 1, an anonymous student left a message on the inner door of the chapel to declare his participation in the escapade. "FLAGPOLE IKE Night of the Great Revolution 1930," the inscription reads. Was this short for Isaac and the student was willing to place his actual name to the deeds done that night? Or maybe the letters are a variation on Julius Caesar's famous proclamation: *iacata alea est* (The die has been cast)! Could IKE be: *iacata kardo est* (the *pole* has been cast)? Or was it an acronym that preceded today's texting shortcuts, and the writer was just telling us he knew the full story (I Know Everything)?

We will certainly never know everything about this turbulent event or who took a hand in it, but the fact that someone bothered to photograph the scene and record the details helps it stand out as the most memorable of Bowdoin College pranks. There have certainly been many others over the years. What is perhaps most curious is how students of today seem to think along very similar lines to their predecessors. A February 2009 edition of the student newspaper, the *Bowdoin Orient*, asked some students, "If you could pull a senior prank and get away with it, what would it be?" One student suggested "putting cows on the third floor of Hubbard." Another suggested "steal[ing] the '09 banner and put it on one of the chapel towers."

Both excellent ideas, but neither is original, I'm afraid! The cow idea was done all the way back in the 1880s and was told to the college newspaper by a local Brunswick man, Leon B. Strout, who remembered the incident from when he was a boy. A faculty member actually kept a cow and calf at that time (faculty regularly kept cows, horses and chickens in those days) and let them graze on the quadrangle during the day. A group of students "borrowed" the bovine pair and led them up the stairs of Appleton Hall, taking them all the way up to the attic. The livestock were discovered when the cow kicked out a window, and the calf was seen sticking its head out to survey the scene. When the authorities went to collect the cows, they discovered that the students had dressed the cow in pajamas and a nightcap. They had also given the calf a nightcap to wear, but its mother had already started eating that. Strout mentions another prank in which students took all the china from Appleton Hall and strung it along some clothesline and suspended it from the roof of that dormitory to the nearest spire of the chapel. Even more comical, the Bowdoin staff, furious upon seeing this suspended crockery and deciding they had no interest in risking broken necks trying to get the objects down, got their hands on a shotgun and brought the whole apparatus down to earth with a few well-aimed blasts.

The placing of a class banner on a spire of the chapel has been successfully managed five times, according to Louis C. Hatch's definitive *History of Bowdoin College*. Jonathan P. Ciley (1891) and George B. Chandler (1890) both unfurled their class flags there in 1888. Donald B. MacMillan, of the class of 1897 (of Bowdoin's Peary MacMillan Artic Museum), and Charles D. Moulton (1898) followed suit a few years later. A member of the class of 1908 was the last person to scale the chapel and plant the class banner, but no one took credit for that final performance. Fortunately, no one has attempted this prank lately, and it would be far more difficult today as both of the towers were completely rebuilt and restored in 2005. The many handy fissures and cracks that once might have made usable toeholds for a venturesome student are gone.

No collection of Bowdoin College student antics would be complete without a mention of the *Great Temple Explosion of 1875*. The "temple" in this case was the euphemism used by students to refer to the college outhouse.

A number of students decided that the administration had allowed the standards of this facility to fall so low that they had no choice but to obliterate this eyesore once and for all. An 1877 alumnus admitted to the act he and his cohorts perpetrated at his fiftieth reunion, and the *Bowdoin Alumnus* printed excerpts of his confession in 1926:

> *We filled the kettle with powder—how much of it I don't remember—and ran the fuse into it through the spout. We fastened the lid down with heavy wire and wrapped yards of rope about the whole thing, finally making it a big, solid white mass by dressing it with liquid plaster of Paris, which quickly hardened. In the silent hours of early morning, we lowered this engine of destruction into the center of the "Temple's" pit, lighted the 20-foot-long fuse and stole back to our virtuous beds.*

The violence of the explosion shocked even the youths who had planted the device. It shook the entire campus, and the building they despised was completely leveled.

College records show that running water was not installed in at least one of the dormitories until 1892, so we can only assume the conditions of the Temple must have been poor indeed if the prospect of *no* outhouse seemed better to these students than making do with the only one they had.

Chapter 7

SECURITY CONCERNS

We meet them at the doorway, on the stair,
Along the passages they come and go...

A library is supposed to be quiet, but if you have ever been in the stacks of Hubbard Hall at night, you know that it can also be rather unnerving. A cough or a dropped book seems to break a silence that is best left undisturbed, and the looming shelves and dust-darkened windows seem to frown down on you with displeasure. The translucent mica floors reveal distorted images of levels above and below you and cast strange lights around you.

Built in 1903 to replace the college library located in Bannister Hall, only the back portion of the building retains that role today. Sealed off from the main part of Hubbard Hall, the only public access to the "Stacks" is via an underground tunnel connected to the newer Hawthorne-Longfellow Library. As you travel down the tunnel, you can easily spot where the new crosses over to the old. All six floors of the Hubbard Stacks have remained relatively unchanged and contain volumes that have rested on the same shelves for over one hundred years.

A staff member from Bowdoin's Office of Security has the job of securing the stacks every night and making sure that no one has stayed behind before he or she locks up the building for the night. One night, an officer took the elevator to the sixth floor, walked through and then took the elevator to the fifth floor. After scanning that floor, she was headed back to the elevator when she saw it being called up to the sixth floor. This meant someone on

A view of the Hubbard Stacks demonstrating the translucent floors and ceilings. *Holly Sherburne.*

Exterior view of the Hubbard Stacks. *Holly Sherburne.*

the sixth floor had pushed the button to call it up there. She realized she must have missed a student somehow, and he or she was just now leaving.

She heard the elevator doors open and close on the sixth floor, so she pushed the call button again so it would stop on the fifth floor and she could escort the student out of the locked building. When the doors opened on the fifth floor, no one was there.

Two more officers were called in to check the entire building. They started at the top and worked their way down to the fourth floor without finding anyone. Then they looked and saw the elevator being called back up to the sixth floor again. One officer ran up the stairs, one ran down the stairs to cover the exit and the original officer pushed the call button on the fourth floor and waited.

Again, the doors opened, and no one was there.

A work order was placed to check the elevator. The electricians came back and said it was in perfect working order.

Chapter 8

HAUNTED HOUSES

All houses wherein men have lived and died
Are haunted houses...

When you first walk through the open doors of Bowdoin's library, you are immediately greeted with portraits of the men for whom the building is named: Henry Wadsworth Longfellow and Nathaniel Hawthorne, perhaps the most famous of Bowdoin College's many illustrious alumni.

Longfellow came to Bowdoin at the age of fifteen in the fall of 1822. After graduating Bowdoin, he accepted a position in the Bowdoin faculty and taught there for a number of years, but after several trips to Europe, he settled down in Cambridge, Massachusetts, as a professor of modern languages at Harvard and simultaneously became the most celebrated of American poets in his day. He rented rooms at a home near Cambridge called the Craigie House, whose previous great claim to fame had been as the headquarters for General George Washington during the British assault on Boston in 1775. Later, when Longfellow married his second wife, his father-in-law bought the entire home for Longfellow as a wedding gift, and the great poet lived out the rest of his life (forty-five years altogether) in this house, writing the bulk of his most famous works, including *Paul Revere's Ride*, *The Song of Hiawatha* and the *Courtship of Miles Standish*.

Longfellow writes that all houses are haunted houses, but because of some strange occurrences, his house actually became an official haunted house—or at least a copy did. Such was Longfellow's literary popularity

Portrait of Henry Wadsworth Longfellow
in the Hawthorne Longfellow Library.
Holly Sherburne.

The "Longfellow House" in Minneapolis, now seeing better days as an interpretive center
for the local parks office. *Bobamnertiopsis (Wikipedia).*

that even his house became famous. Sears, Roebuck and Company sold blueprints of it, and many replicas of his home started appearing across the nation. In 1907, a rather odd businessman from Minneapolis built a replica of the Longfellow house to live in for himself, as well as creating a zoo that he called the Longfellow Zoological Gardens. After this man's death, the house became a branch of the Minneapolis Public Library but closed in 1968 and was basically unused until the 1980s, when once a year, a local civic group used it as a haunted house attraction.

Longfellow has another association with haunted residences, and it is connected to one of his most famous collections of poetry: *Tales of a Wayside Inn*. Longfellow wrote this collection of poetry as an attempt to recover from his wife's death a year earlier and as a way to take his mind off his worries about his eldest son serving in the Civil War as a soldier in the Army of the Potomac. The inn that inspired this work was an establishment he visited in 1862 with a friend. In the prelude to the work, Longfellow describes the inn:

> *A kind of old hobgoblin hall,*
> *Now somewhat fallen to decay,*
> *With weather-stains upon the wall,*
> *And stairways worn, and crazy doors,*
> *And creaking and uneven floors,*
> *And chimneys huge, and tiled and tall.*

An apt description of a haunted house if ever there was one. Built in 1707, in Sudbury, Massachusetts, the Red Horse Tavern, as it was known then, already had a deep history filled with a number of ghost stories when Longfellow visited it in 1862. The most popularly known ghost is that of Jerusha Howe, a resident of the inn in the 1700s who fell in love with a man from Britain. The man left her with promises to come back and marry her, but he was never seen in America again. She lived another forty-four years in the inn pining for her lost lover and apparently waits for him still after death. According to the inn's website, the rooms where she lived (#9 and #10) are the most haunted parts of the building. People report seeing her appear in their rooms or even slipping into bed with them.

Chapter 9

DARK FAMILY SECRETS

Of earthly wants and aspirations high,
Come from the influence of an unseen star

Returning back to the Bowdoin College Library, we now bring our attention to the opposite wall of the entry from Longfellow's portrait. There hangs the portrait of Nathaniel Hawthorne, less illustrious in his time than Longfellow but now probably Bowdoin's most famous alumnus. Among his many other literary accomplishments, one could make the case that Hawthorne was one of the greatest influences of the horror genre in American literature. Edgar Allan Poe, H.P. Lovecraft and Stephen King have all acknowledged Hawthorne's influence on their work.

That Hawthorne should be one of the originators of American Gothic and horror is no surprise if you consider his own origins. Hawthorne was born in Salem, Massachusetts, in 1804. He was not simply a resident of this infamous town but also related to some of the town's most notorious characters. Hawthorne was a direct descendant of the legendary William Hathorne, a self-made man who arrived in America in 1630 and rose to become a deputy of the General Court of Massachusetts. Hathorne was a dogged champion for the rights and freedoms of Puritans who had come to the New World to escape persecution, but he certainly didn't feel those liberties should be extended to other faiths that had likewise sought religious opportunity here. He was the quintessential, hard-minded Puritan for whom compassion or consideration was never to be wasted on infidels. As such,

The portrait of Nathaniel Hawthorne that greets visitors to the Hawthorne-Longfellow Library. *Holly Sherburne.*

he made himself famous for having Quakers publicly whipped through the streets of Salem if any ever dared to set foot on Puritan land.

William's son, John Hathorne, was one of the first three magistrates who presided over the witchcraft trials, which eventually resulted in the executions of twenty men and women. Beyond his real-life involvement in the shameful witch trails, writers have latched onto the character of John Hathorne as the main protagonist in the terrible event. In Arthur Miller's *The Crucible*, Hathorne is an outright sadist, clearly relishing the task of judging and condemning his victims. In his play *Giles Corey of the Salem Farms*, Henry Wadsworth Longfellow portrays Hathorne as a zealot who cares little about the dangers of wrongly persecuting the innocent in his quest to dispel the devil from his province. While Cotton Mather encourages him to tread with care so that individual rights are upheld, Hathorne rebukes him with:

> For one, I do not fear excess of zeal.
> What do we gain by parleying with the Devil?
> You reason, but you hesitate to act!
> Ah, reverend sir! believe me, in such cases
> The only safety is in acting promptly.
> 'T is not the part of wisdom to delay
> In things where not to do is still to do
> A deed more fatal than the deed we shrink from.
> You are a man of books and meditation,
> But I am one who acts.

Later in the play, Hathorne presides over Giles Corey's examination, and when Corey refuses to enter any plea to the accusation of being a warlock, the old farmer is taken out of town and pressed to death by having rocks piled on a board placed over his naked body. The play covers the true story of Giles Corey. His wife was hanged for witchcraft, but he could not be compelled to acknowledge his accusers. As they piled more rocks on his chest in an attempt to illicit a plea from him, Corey would only respond famously: "More weight!" Because he did not enter a plea, he could not be tried, and although that didn't prevent his death, by refusing to submit to the Salem courts, his sons were able to keep his lands and wealth, which would otherwise have been taken from them if their father had been convicted.

In *The Devil and Daniel Webster*, Stephen Vincent Benet has Satan choose John Hathorne as the judge to try the case of Jabez Stone's immortal soul against the claims of the Devil. "Justice Hathorne is a jurist of experience," the demon notes. "He presided at certain witch trials once held in Salem. There were others who repented of the business later, but not he."

In this matter, the Devil speaks truly, for after the hysteria of the witch hunts had passed, most of those involved with the persecutions admitted wrongdoing and asked for forgiveness. John Hale, a minister present at many of the proceedings, wrote, "Such was the darkness of that day, the tortures and lamentations of the afflicted, and the power of former presidents, that we walked in the clouds, and could not see our way." Samuel Sewer accepted "the Blame & Shame" of his role. Even Ann Putnam Jr., one of the original accusers who began the madness, offered a heartfelt public apology. The repentance of John Hathorne is conspicuously absent from these litanies of regrets.

Nathaniel Hawthorne was fascinated and even disturbed by John Hathorne's behavior and the behavior of all his ancestors. In his most famous works, you will find righteous figures of authority using their alleged piety to mask their darker natures and to abuse the weak and defenseless. *The Scarlet Letter* certainly echoes the fervor of a witch hunt, and *The House of Seven Gables* intermixes contemporary dishonesty and scandal with the accused witches and their prosecutors from the past. In this work, Hawthorne has Matthew Maul, accused of witchcraft by the lofty Colonel Pyncheon so he may steal the innocent man's land, stare down at his enemy from the gallows and speak this warning: "God will give him blood to drink!"

Hawthorne borrowed this line from a real quote from the Salem witch trials. When the Reverend Nicholas Noyes pronounced Sara Good guilty, she shouted back, "I am no more a witch than you are a wizard! Take away my life and God will give you blood to drink."

Twenty-five years later, the Reverend Nicholas Noyes died of a hemorrhage in his neck, choking on his own blood, a fate that Hawthorne assigns to Colonel Pyncheon and his equally corrupt descendant Judge Pyncheon years later.

Less well known among Hawthorne's works is the short story "Young Goodman Brown," also set during the era of the Salem trials with visions of witches' covens and demons imaginative enough to shock even the modern reader. Stephen King called the piece "one of the ten best stories written by an American" and used it as part of his inspiration for his own short story "The Man in the Black Suit."

In the story, Goodman Brown dares to keep an appointment with the Devil, leaving behind his dear wife and venturing into the gloom of the forest. There he comes across a man "in grave and decent attire" who is quickly revealed to be Satan himself, though in many ways he has contrived to make himself appear as Goodman Brown's own father. Goodman Brown attempts to defy the demon's attempts to seduce him to evil by invoking the long-held good name of his family, but the Devil responds with a different version of Brown's family history that seems to come straight from Hawthorne's own unease about his ancestors:

A scene from the Salem witch trials. The standing figure with arm raised is thought to be Mary Wolcott, one of the witnesses at the trials. *Witchcraft at Salem Village*, taken from William A. Crafts's *Pioneers in the Settlement of America: From Florida in 1510 to California in 1849. Wikipedia.*

> *I have been as well acquainted with your family as with ever a one among the Puritans; and that's no trifle to say. I helped your grandfather, the constable, when he lashed the Quaker woman so smartly through the streets of Salem; and it was I that brought your father a pitch-pine knot, kindled at my own hearth, to set fire to an Indian village, in King Philip's war. They were my good friends, both; and many a pleasant walk have we had along this path, and returned merrily after midnight. I would fain be friends with you for their sake.*

With this revelation, the Devil provides more evidence that all the people the young man thought of as good and pious were, in fact, secretly in league with the demon. During the course of their walk, they spy Goody Cloyse, a good Christian woman who taught young Goodman Brown his prayers when he was a boy. As Brown stands back, the Devil approaches her and greets her as an old friend. To the young man's horror, she reciprocates his greeting, and the two discuss evil potions of "the juice of smallage, and cinquefoil, and wolf's bane…Mingled with fine wheat and the fat of a new-born babe."

Before she vanishes from the scene, the old lady reveals that she is on her way to the Devil's coven where "a nice young man is to be taken into communion." Goodman Brown walks on, and the Devil continues to present arguments to convince the young man to join him. Finally, Brown will walk no farther but sits down on a rock, saying he could not abandon his wife. The Devil leaves him to muse on what he has seen and heard, and Brown shortly sees two preachers he has known and revered pass by him on the way to the coven. One of them mentions that a young woman is also to join their ranks that night. Shortly after this, Brown hears the cries of a woman he takes to be his wife being dragged forcibly to the unholy ceremony. Despairing that his only remaining surety of goodness in the world is about to be sacrificed to evil, Brown is roused from his seat and madly flies toward the spot where the people are gathering.

Upon arriving at the wicked scene, young Goodman Brown strides forth when the Devil cries, "Bring forth the converts!" Brown is joined by a young veiled woman he knows to be his wife. Satan orders the two inductees to turn and gaze on the motley congregation and see that all that they thought was holy has, in fact, been in his service all along. The demon then makes this terrifying speech:

> *Ye deemed them holier than yourselves, and shrank from your own sin, contrasting it with their lives of righteousness and prayerful aspirations heavenward. Yet here are they all in my worshipping assembly. This night it shall be granted you to know their secret deeds: how hoary-bearded elders of the church have whispered wanton words to the young maids of their households; how many a woman, eager for widows' weeds, has given her husband a drink at bedtime and let him sleep his last sleep in her bosom; how beardless youths have made haste to inherit their fathers' wealth; and how fair damsels—blush not, sweet ones—have dug little graves in the garden, and bidden me, the sole guest to an infant's funeral.*

The Devil has Brown stare at his wife and says to them both, "Ye had still hoped that virtue were not all a dream. Now are ye undeceived. Evil is the nature of mankind. Evil must be your only happiness. Welcome again, my children, to the communion of your race."

Then, just as the Devil is preparing to anoint them both with blood from a pool at the center of the forest glade, Goodman Brown finds the strength to resist one last time, and immediately he finds himself alone in the forest with all demonic activity vanished.

In a dark twist to the usual parable of good resisting the forces of evil, when Goodman Brown returns to his village, he does not do so as a hero who has faced down evil and is rewarded with a blessed life for his faithfulness. Rather, what the Devil has shown to him so shakes the young man that he lives out the remainder of his days unsure of what is real and what is false, what is good and what is evil. He cannot be sure if pastors are sincere or hypocrites. He doesn't know if his neighbors are in league with Satan or if Satan just wants him to believe that. He isn't even sure of his own wife. He can no longer attend church services because the gatherings remind him too much of the witches' coven of his vision. For the rest of his life, he is "a stern, a sad, a darkly meditative, a distrustful, if not desperate man."

This dark study of the nature of good and evil seems to echo Hawthorne's own uncertainly about the ability of man to comprehend real goodness in a physical world. The result is both a horror story and psychological thriller that seems far ahead of its time.

So if you enjoy a good horror story, you may wish to reflect how much you owe to the imaginations and anxieties of Bowdoin's own Nathaniel Hawthorne. And if you haven't found a reason to read one of Hawthorne's works since reading *The Scarlet Letter* in your high school American literature class, treat yourself to the *House of Seven Gables* or *Young Goodman Brown*.

Chapter 10

THE ECHOING FOOTSTEPS

Across whose trembling planks our fancies crowd
Into the realm of mystery and night—

Although only one of three Medieval Revival buildings on the college quadrangle, the Mary Frances Searles Science Building with its crenellated turrets, castle-like façade and distinct yellow brick stands out as its own unique structure. Like Hubbard Hall, the Gothic trappings of the roof and towers make it easy to imagine the Searles Science Building as the ideal setting for a ghost story, but it is perhaps the odd history of the people behind its construction that most stirs the imagination.

Mary Frances Searles was the widow of Mark Hopkins, one of the four principal owners of the Central Pacific Railroad. In 1887, just three years after her husband's death, Mary married Edward F. Searles, a man twenty-two years her junior whom she had contracted to work on the interiors of her mansions. The newlyweds took up residence in Great Barrington, Massachusetts, in the lavish Barrington House, more commonly known thereafter as Searles Castle.

Mary was easily one of the richest women in America, so her second marriage at age sixty-seven certainly raised many eyebrows. The couple settled down to a quiet and private life, but that didn't prevent rumors and hints of scandal. Servants' gossip had it that Searles was trying to frighten his wife to death, moving furniture around at night to upset and disturb her. There were also stories of secret passageways that Searles had constructed

Mary Frances Searles Science Building. No building on Bowdoin's campus houses more intrigue. *Holly Sherburne.*

in the castle to provide him easy access to the maids' quarters while his wife was sleeping. The worst rumor of all was that Searles and a chambermaid had worked in concert to poison Mrs. Searles, though her death had been ruled a result of natural causes. Not surprisingly, Searles Castle is purported to be haunted by all three individuals.

The aftermath of her death in 1891 only brought about more attention and scandal when the contents of Mrs. Searles's will was made public. The old lady had almost entirely disinherited her adopted son Timothy and left all her fortune to Edward.

At this point, the reader may be asking how the characters in this history came to be associated with Bowdoin College. Neither Mrs. Searles nor either of her husbands had any strong ties to that esteemed establishment, so how did a building bearing her name come to grace this campus? The impetus for this relationship came from Timothy Hopkins, the disinherited adopted son, who took up a legal challenge to contest the will that had left Edward all of her immense wealth. To argue against this challenge, Edward Searles retained Thomas Hamlin Hubbard, graduate of the Bowdoin College class of 1857. Hubbard succeeded in winning the case for Searles, with Hopkins accepting a settlement of a few million. More than $50 million and a quarter ownership of the Central Pacific Railroad remained in Searles's hands. Not surprisingly, when Hubbard heard of his college's need for a new science building, he found a willing donor in his grateful client. Searles commissioned Henry Vaughn, who had overseen the work on Searles Castle, to be the architect for building, and in 1894, the Mary Frances Searles Science Building was dedicated, and Bowdoin College had a science facility to compete with any college in New England.

The general public has long forgotten the stains of scandal, but the old building has managed over the years to form a reputation of its own. Tim French, a longtime employee of Bowdoin's Facilities Department, says Searles is "the noisiest building on campus," and most of its residents agree. Searles is a hard building to work in at night because it makes so many unexplained noises. You might be wrapped up in some experiment or math problem in complete silence when suddenly—*bang!*—an unexplained noise breaks you from your reverie. Was it a water pipe? Some shifting plaster cracking on the floor above you? Who can say?

Searles Castle, Great Barrington, Massachusetts. A source of unspeakable deeds or just ugly rumor? *John Phelan, 2012 (Wikipedia).*

Outside of its general noisiness, Searles has one particular sound that has disturbed its occupants for years. When walking through the long hallways, people report hearing footsteps behind them as though someone was right on their heels. When they turn around, no one is there—except that a few people have said they have seen a white, shadowy figure darting away out of the corner of their eyes. The figure has also been seen in the basement hallway, where a number of people have said they felt there was some presence with them when they were down there alone. A custodian working in the building complained of hearing voices and finally had to leave her job because of the incidents.

The first-floor hallway in Searles where some spirit still walks. *Holly Sherburne.*

One legend has it that the shadowy figure is the ghost of a town girl who fell from one of the turrets when Searles Hall was being built, but research of the newspapers from that time finds no mention of such an accident. More say that the figure, and the heavy tread you can hear, belongs to the spirit of a custodian who worked in the building for years.

Given its unique origins, it's easy to imagine a ghost feeling comfortable setting up an eternal residence in the old building.

Chapter 11

BOWDOIN'S MYSTERIOUS HERMIT

Our little lives are kept in equipoise
By opposite attractions and desires;

On a summer day in 1840, two men came to Brunswick with hopes of earning some money from the residents by way of puppet show performances. Their previous stop had been in Portland, and they likely had heard that Brunswick, with its young Bowdoin gentlemen, would offer a solid opportunity to gather a sizable audience.

History does not record how the exhibition was received, but it could not have been a great success. One of the men soon left town, and the other, Thomas Curtis, quickly abandoned his theatrical equipage and set himself up as a mender of clothes for the townspeople and Bowdoin students. According to his obituary in the *Brunswick Telegraph*, Curtis quickly learned that he could make even more money as "a man of all work, at the College, doing errands, carrying up wood, beating carpets."

Although he remained employed at Bowdoin for the next twenty-seven years, little more is known for certain about Curtis and his origins than what has been revealed above. Of his history, Curtis would reveal almost nothing and would become angry if anyone inquired too deeply about his past. Such reticence only encouraged the imagination of the young Bowdoin gentlemen, and they began to form various theories about this mysterious character who had appeared on their campus.

There was a report that Curtis was born in England and that he had lost the love of his life to the affections of his own brother, leaving him a broken

Bowdoin College as it looked in the last years of Diogenes's lifetime. *From Louis C. Hatch,* The History of Bowdoin College.

and embittered man. His 1868 obituary refers to him as "an inveterate woman-hater" and a heavy drinker. Certainly something had happened to this man and brought him down in the world, and many students felt he must have once been a professional man, as his work with clothing was so fine. And while he did not seem to have been greatly educated, he was a passionate reader and collector of books. Indeed, all his wages appeared to go to either books or his more unfortunate addiction.

Although often gruff and surly, Curtis could be courteous if treated respectfully and would at times surprise students with quotations and an encyclopedic knowledge on certain topics. When his thoughtful and cautionary poem "Morning, Spring Term, 1864" appeared in the *Brunswick Telegraph* just four years before his own death, the students of Bowdoin must have smiled and nodded, "That's our Diogenes."

The students had taken to calling Curtis "Diogenes" early on in his tenure at Bowdoin, and he certainly shared many of that legendary philosopher's traits. Like Diogenes, Curtis had arrived in town with another man who abandoned him, and thereafter Thomas Curtis lived in abject poverty in a small shack that could not have been much more refined than Diogenes of Sinope's famous tub in the Athens marketplace. Doubtless seeing this odd character traveling up the hill from his shack carrying his lantern in the dim light of dawn to start his work turned the

Right: Thomas A. Curtis, aka "Diogenes." *Bowdoin College Archives, Brunswick, Maine.*

Below: Diogenes's humble dwelling just off campus. *Bowdoin College Archives, Brunswick, Maine.*

young scholars' minds to ideas of a wizened philosopher coming to them in search of "an honest man."

An autograph album from the class of 1849 with many stories of warmth and appreciation for their odd caretaker demonstrates how this mysterious and reclusive man had enriched their life. The young gentlemen who wrote in his book repeat two words in almost every entry: honorable and mysterious. "Over you hangs a mystery," one man writes. "I have asked you several times to solve it, but you as often evade the question."

The students on several occasions offered to take up funds to buy Curtis a new house closer to the campus, but the private old man always refused. Curtis lived alone in his shack for almost thirty years. When he died, it was discovered that his humble dwelling contained a collection of two thousand books. Curtis had always stated to incredulous students that they would one day benefit from his legacy and even had a practice of assessing incoming freshmen twenty-five cents as investment for their futures. Diogenes left no will, but since he had never revealed enough about himself that they could hope to find any surviving relations, the college added the Thomas A. Curtis collection to its own growing library.

Chapter 12

THE LAUGHING PORTRAIT

*The stranger at my fireside cannot see
The forms I see, nor hear the sounds I hear*

A good way to win a bet with a visitor to the Bowdoin campus is to ask if they can guess which of the college's buildings was actually built in a different state. If they happen to guess (correctly) that it was Massachusetts Hall, you might offer them a chance to double their winnings if they can guess how it was moved to Maine.

The answer, of course, is that it was never moved at all. When Massachusetts Hall was built in 1802, Maine was still eighteen years away from acquiring official statehood and was still a part of the state of Massachusetts. So, technically speaking, Massachusetts Hall was built in Massachusetts and "moved" to Maine overnight on March 15, 1820, when, as part of the Missouri Compromise, Maine separated from Massachusetts and became its own state.

Massachusetts Hall is Bowdoin College's oldest building by twenty years with the second-oldest being Winthrop Hall. Some records might lead you to believe that Maine Hall is older than Winthrop, but those records refer to the original Maine Hall built in 1808 (also in Massachusetts) that burned down in 1822. The college had intended Maine Hall to be its first construction, but financial difficulties forced it to proceed with Massachusetts Hall's smaller footprint.

For the first six years of Bowdoin College's existence, Massachusetts Hall *was* the college. It was the president's home and office, classroom

Massachusetts Hall. *Author's collection.*

building, library and dormitory. In 1805, a separate house was built for the president roughly in the area where the Searles Science Building stands today. In 1808, Maine Hall took over as the college dormitory, leaving Massachusetts Hall to just its academic and administrative tasks. In 1844, the newly built Bannister Hall housed the college's library, but Massachusetts Hall went on to serve as the office for the president until the latter half of the twentieth century.

Despite having the deepest history of all of Bowdoin's buildings, Massachusetts Hall has been slow to give up its ghost stories. For the first five years that I gave the Haunted Tour, I would walk past the building in silence until someone in the audience would say, "What about Mass Hall? It *must* have stories!" I would answer that I felt it must have some and I was certainly on the lookout for them, but so far no one had come forward with any. Finally, a few years ago, the stories started to come in.

The best story involves a student studying in the first-floor seminar room one night when he was alone in the building. The student was working late to finish a paper that was due the following morning, but despite the urgency of his task, as the hours rolled on, he felt the need for a break and rested his head down on the old table he was using. Of course, before long he was fast asleep.

The young man didn't know for how long he had dozed off, but he was suddenly startled out of his sleep by a peal of deep laughter that seemed to be right in front of him. The student sat straight up in his chair, and his gaze fell on the portrait of Joshua Lawrence Chamberlain that hangs directly above the room's old fireplace. The student got out of his chair, searched the building and verified that no one else was there. He went back to the seminar room and stared at the portrait again. He couldn't help but feel there was a connection.

Joshua Lawrence Chamberlain was certainly familiar with this room where his portrait now hangs. As a student at Bowdoin (class of 1852) and later as a professor of modern languages, he no doubt had interactions with President Leonard Woods when he held office there. Following his impressive career in the Civil War and politics, Chamberlain took up the office himself as president of the college from 1871 to 1883.

Great champion of education that he was, it is easy to imagine Chamberlain's spirit feeling compelled to take action to startle a youth

Massachusetts Hall seminar room. The portrait of Chamberlain and the mysterious locking door are in the back of the room. *Holly Sherburne.*

from slumber so he would return to his studies. However, laughter does seem an odd way for this dignified and revered alumnus to make his wishes known. And the other story connected to this room seems so out of character for Chamberlain that we might conclude he cannot be the source of this strange activity.

To the left of the portrait and fireplace in this room, there is an old wooden door that leads to the back door of Massachusetts Hall and a small bathroom just beyond that. This door once had an old-fashioned iron bar that had to be manually raised and set into a latch in order to lock it. A professor was working late in his office one night when the building was locked up and empty, and he got up for a restroom break. He left his office and crossed through the old seminar room, through this door and on to the bathroom. After he had been inside for only a minute, he suddenly heard the seminar door slam shut and the iron bar being thrown into place. He stepped out into the landing, and sure enough, the door was solidly locked. He had fortunately brought his keys with him, but even so, he had to walk out the back door and go outside around the building and let himself back in via the front door to get back to his office. He met no one on his way back in and went on to verify that he was the only person there.

Massachusetts Hall has too rich a past and too long a list of residents in its illustrious two-hundred-year history for us to say with any certainly whose spirit is responsible for these stories. Eight presidents, dozens of faculty members and thousands of students have used the old building as living quarters, office spaces or classrooms. We can only hope that since Massachusetts Hall has started revealing some of its stories, we will soon have more to share.

Chapter 13

BOWDOIN'S BIT OF MACABRE

So from the world of spirits there descends...

If there is a main attraction for *Haunted Bowdoin College* then it must surely be Adams Hall. No other building has such a rich history of the paranormal—and is it any wonder? From 1861 until 1920, Adams Hall was the home of the Maine Medical School and, as such, had a steady stream of bodies being brought through its doors for dissection. Many of the bodies were shipped from Maryland, where at the time grave-robbing laws were lax and an unscrupulous fellow could make a deal for quick cash from a doctor who didn't ask too many questions. Penitentiaries and poor houses were the most common sources for this grisly trade since in the first case, no one might even care to claim the body of a convicted felon and in the second, destitute and desperate families might be only too happy to make use of an opportunity to recover costs incurred while tending to a long-ailing relative.

Step in through the main doors of Adams Hall, and you enter a small foyer with the door to the basement to your left and a stairway just beyond leading to the upper floors. If you pass through the basement door, you will go down to where the cadavers were kept "in pickle" until they were ready for use. You can still see the alcoves (now plastered in) where the bodies were slid into the walls to be kept out of the way.

Take a few steps forward, and you will see the stairs winding up above you. Take a look at the shape of the space around the stairs—just perfect for hoisting a gurney. And that is just what they used to do. The dissection

The old medical school in Adams Hall. *From* Class of 1876 *(Bowdoin College yearbook).*

Adams Hall basement, where bodies were kept prior to dissection. The white, plastered-in areas were once cubby holes for cadaver storage. *Holly Sherburne.*

rooms were on the top floor of Adams, and a hook in the ceiling was used to hoist the bodies to the top floor. You can still see the hook today if you look straight up to the top landing.

When Adams Hall was renovated in 2007 (sadly, removing forever a lot of its spooky charm), workers on the project made a gruesome discovery. When pulling up the floorboards on the top floor, they discovered that some of the boards were actually lids to the coffins that were used to ship those corpses used for medical research. You can even read a number on one of the lids that must once have identified the otherwise nameless soul who had been shipped to Maine following his demise. The discovery is a wonderful connection to the old medical school and a reminder of the old saying that has been called "the four threads of New England character": "Eat it up. Wear it out. Make it do. Go without."

In the early days of Bowdoin College, throwing away perfecting usable lumber like coffin lids would be unthinkable and probably didn't seem remotely odd or creepy at the time.

Not surprisingly, Adams Hall is a rite of passage for new security guards joining the force at Bowdoin. Former security officer Louann Dustin-Hunter tells how a rookie guard was assigned the task of securing Adams Hall on his first night on the job. She and her partner left the rookie at the door of the old building and then moved on to the other side of campus. After a short while, they got a message over the radio from their new colleague: "Very funny!" he said. They looked back across the quad to Adams Hall and saw that all the lights in the building had gone dark. When they met up with the man later, he accused them of playing a trick on him, but they had been all the way on the other side of campus when he was stepping through the hallways and rooms of the old building.

Long after serving as a morgue for the medical school, the college found other uses for the Adams Hall cellar. Only a few years ago, the area was accessible to the public and was used as costume storage for Pickard Theater and also contained a small study room. Getting to the costume shop required walking past the cadaver walls in the dark before you could get to a light. A student went down one night to retrieve a costume, and as she was heading toward the light switch, she saw just ahead of her a dark shape hunched over by the wall. She waited for her eyes to adjust to the dark so she could make sense of what she was seeing, but rather than clearing up, the figure continued to become less and less solid. She stayed long enough to watch it melt away into nothing and then turned around and ran back up the stairs and straight back to her room.

The stairwell of Adams Hall. The hook can be seen as a black dot in the center of the picture. *Holly Sherburne.*

A coffin lid used as flooring discovered in the Adams Hall 2007 renovation. *Photo by Holly Sherburne. Coffin lid courtesy of Bowdoin College Archives, Brunswick, Maine.*

A few years before that, students were using the study room during one stormy night. In the middle of their session, there was a sudden clap of thunder and the building lost power. The students were instantly encased in complete darkness. As the students started groping their way toward the door, they were stopped by the appearance of a bluish-white light that kept bobbing back and forth by the doorway. The students watched in silence until the light finally faded and the power came back on.

One night about thirty years ago, an ambulance was seen pulling up outside of Adams Hall. As a custodian was wheeled out on a stretcher, he could be heard repeating over and over again: "I was pushed!" He had been found by a co-worker at the bottom of the stairs when he had been left alone in the building. Another custodian told how, while vacuuming the third floor, his vacuum cleaner suddenly stopped. Thinking he must have accidentally jarred the plug from the outlet, he followed the cord back. When he got there, the cord was firmly plugged in. What's more, as he stood there, the vacuum cleaner suddenly jumped back to life, nearly causing the custodian to jump out of his skin.

On the third floor only a few years ago, an employee was coming into her office late one night to finish a project. When she got to her door, it was locked, so she got out her key and inserted it into the lock. No sooner had she done so than the entire door started shaking violently. Being a rather brave person, she went ahead and unlocked the door, thinking she was going to find one of her office mates inside playing a trick on her. When she opened the door, she found the office completely deserted. The project would have to wait, she decided. She went straight home, and she never worked in Adams Hall after dark ever again.

And what about the top floor where the dissections actually occurred? Well, a person in facilities shared a story about that room that he couldn't explain. On this particular night, a storm had cut power to not just Bowdoin but to all of Brunswick and Topsham as well. He came to campus when that happened because back then if they didn't shut off the power circuits in the buildings, when the power came back on suddenly, it would sometimes blow them out. He had just come from the basement where he had removed the fuses and was heading for his truck when he looked back and saw a strange light coming from the window of the top floor. This made no sense to him because there was no power in the building—no power in the entire city! So what could be causing the light? Knowing Adams Hall's reputation for the unusual, he decided he didn't really want to walk up five floors alone in the darkened building to check it out. He reasoned it out to me, saying, "I'm an electrician and I knew there was no electricity in that building. So whatever was making that light was none of my business!"

He got into his truck and drove home.

The top floor of Adams Hall, the location of the dissection rooms and the source of an unexplained light. *Author's collection.*

Medical students posing with their favorite cadaver. *Bowdoin College Archives, Brunswick, Maine.*

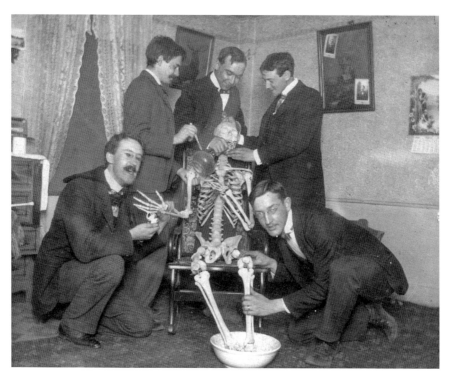

Medical students posing with their "first patient." *Bowdoin College Archives, Brunswick, Maine.*

Today, Adams Hall houses Bowdoin College's Environmental Sciences and Sociology and Anthropology Departments. On a tour I gave a few years ago sponsored by the Office of Admissions, I had a number of high school students who were considering attending Bowdoin. At the conclusion of the tour, I asked if anyone had any questions or comments. A young lady spoke up and said, "I enjoyed the tour, but I was planning on coming here as an environmental studies major, and I'm not sure I can deal with Adams Hall." On that particular night, Adams Hall had decided to perform for us (as it frequently does). While we were alone in the building and I was describing the goings-on in the basement area, a dull knocking sound started coming from one of the walls where the cadavers used to be stored.

"You're doing that!" one of the students said to me nervously.

"I'm afraid not," I replied. "But this sort of thing does happen sometimes when I am down here. It usually goes away on its own."

"Well, how about we get out of here before we upset it further?" he suggested.

I hope those students were able to put aside their concerns and still decided to enroll at Bowdoin. I do sometimes wonder about the wisdom of having me give these tours to prospective students.

Chapter 14

THE PARTY IS *NOT OVER*

Wafts through these earthly mists and vapors dense
A vital breath of more ethereal air.

The building now known simply as "85 Federal" began its days as the home of Captain Francis C. Jordan and certainly didn't start with its current name because, when it was constructed in 1860, it resided a few houses farther northwest at 77 Federal Street. The house was moved to its current location on the corner of Federal and Bath Streets in 1874 to create an extensive garden space at its previous location. The exterior of the building has been well preserved and still has the cupola that was common in Italianate architecture. In coastal New England towns such as Brunswick, these cupolas were called "widow's walks" or "captain's walks" and were thought to be built either for captains' wives to watch for their husbands returning from sea or for captains to watch over their shipping endeavors.

From 1867 until 1992, 85 Federal was the home for Bowdoin presidents (with a few exceptions) and was fitted with a number of enhancements to increase its prestige, not the least of which was the addition of a ballroom in 1925. Today, the building is used for offices, but it still retains much of its original charm and character with dramatic staircases, splendid chandeliers and elaborate molding.

Residing in the building longest were President Kenneth M. Sills and his wife, Edith. Sills was president at Bowdoin for thirty-five years, but people typically considered the office a jointly held position with the

85 Federal Street. *Author's collection.*

loving couple working in perfect unison. When Professor Sills announced his intention to marry Edith Lansing Koon shortly after assuming the Bowdoin presidency, his friend Robert Hale remarked to him, "I know she'll be a good wife, and I dare say if you want to take a week off, she can run the college as well as you can."

Edith was born in Hancock, Maryland, in 1889, the daughter of an Episcopalian preacher. She attended Wellesley College in Massachusetts and moved to Portland, Maine, in 1912 to teach high school English and Greek. Kenneth and Edith met in 1913 at a teacher's convention held at Bowdoin College while he was dean and a professor of classical languages. They remained close friends even after she moved to New York City in 1916 to teach Latin at a boarding school and to pursue graduate work at Columbia University in language studies and linguistics. The two exchanged many letters while separated, often in one of the ancient languages they both knew so well. In fact, as the Great War was raging in Europe at this time, a telegraph officer mistook one of these missives as a coded message and forwarded it on to the appropriate authorities for analysis. An investigation commenced, but as Herbert Ross Brown relates in his biography on Kenneth Sills, "instead of discovering a dangerous enemy alien operating from 61 East 77th Street, they found a charming young woman who not only was able to establish her innocence, but also to persuade that even an elementary knowledge of Greek had some value."

When Kenneth Sills assumed the presidency, there were those who worried that the shy and reserved bachelor Sills would not be up to all the societal tasks required of the college's chief administrator, but when he married Edith just five months after becoming president, all such concerns were forever put to rest. In a 1964 edition of the Wellesley alumni magazine, a reviewer notes, "When Edith Sills crossed the threshold of 85 Federal Street, the President's house, Bowdoin entered an era of warm hospitality that matched the high quality of academic excellence for which the college was famous."

The residence at 85 Federal Street became famous for its hospitality, and in turn, Edith and her husband hosted a fair number of famous people. Literary luminaries who dined at the president's home included Pulitzer Prize–winning poet and playwright Edna St. Vincent Millay, famed Irish poet William Butler Yeats, T.S. Eliot and Robert Frost. Historical figures like British logician and activist Bertrand Russell and Randolph Churchill, son of Winston Churchill and a member of Parliament, also attended events in the president's home.

But the hospitality that became Edith's trademark did not extend only to the prestigious and famous. The presidential couple made a point of frequently welcoming students into their home. In the Bowdoin College George J. Mitchell Department of Special Collections and Archives, you can find a transcript of a sweetly nostalgic speech that Edith gave in 1946 entitled "Entertaining Undergraduates." In it, Mrs. Sills relates how she and her husband made a point of being at home one afternoon a week so students and faculty could drop in for tea and conversation. She also explains that they made a point to have dinner with twelve to fifteen freshmen on Sunday evenings until they had dined with everyone in that class. She estimates she must have hosted over 250 such meals (and this was in 1946, with six more years of the Sills presidency still to go). Later in the academic year, the Sillses would welcome the senior class to a formal dinner in the ballroom, where they could "have one last good talk of farewell just with them and ourselves." Edith always made a point of using her best china for these senior dinners because "there is no one whom we would wish to honor more than our Bowdoin seniors."

Perhaps Edith's clearest display of her affection for Bowdoin students is related in how she comforted those students who were forced into an interview with her husband after they had received "major warnings" for failing in their studies. She took pity on their remorseful faces and either triesdto cheer them up or offered them distractions from the impending conference. Despite her obvious elegance and sophistication, there was nothing but genuine and easy affection in Edith for all the students of the college, from the boisterous leaders to the shy introverts.

It is no wonder that, as Brown relates in *Sills of Bowdoin*, the final commencement ceremony of the couple's term in office "turned spontaneously into a mounting tribute to both the Silles [*sic*]." At that commencement, and to the delight of her husband (and to her humble embarrassment), Bowdoin College conferred on Edith Sills an honorary degree of "Doctor of Ease and Graciousness."

Kenneth Sills died only two years after retiring from his presidency, but Edith remained active in civic life and Bowdoin affairs for many more years,

Edith and Kenneth Sills entertaining students at their home. *Bowdoin College Archives, Brunswick, Maine.*

The Torrey Barn in the Cram Alumni House, a popular place for college events. *Holly Sherburne.*

Cram Alumni House hallway. *Holly Sherburne.*

serving on various committees and boards. Following her death in 1978, people would often think about Edith whenever there were parties or events being held at 85 Federal, remembering how she had brought such grace and cheerfulness to such occasions. Several years later, at one such party, a secretary declared she could smell Edith's unique perfume wafting through the room. A short time after that, another person was startled out of his work by a sudden gust of cold air and a feeling that Edith was nearby. After that, reports of strange encounters began to surface, and the legend of Edith's ghost in 85 Federal was born.

In fact, her spirit seems to have gone on to inhabit the Cram Alumni House next door as well. When the attached Torrey Barn is used for events, people say that is when you are most likely to detect Edith's presence. A staff person who stayed on to work alone in the building after a party had been held that night watched with surprise as a door behind her suddenly opened on its own and then closed with a bang. Another staff member in the Cram House says when she is working late she frequently feels she is not alone and that a gentle and benevolent spirit is watching her.

Given her lengthy devotion to the college and the number of young lives she touched with her welcoming presence and generous spirit, it is no wonder that people want to believe Edith is still with them at 85 Federal and Cram Alumni House. Students today can no longer receive Edith's kindly invitations to dinner or have her chaperone a dance in the ballroom, but we can all still make a point to pay her a visit and thank her for all she did. If you are very fortunate, you might even catch a whiff of her perfume and know that she is still looking out for Bowdoin's well-being.

Chapter 15

FLUSHED WITH FEAR

The harmless phantoms on their errands glide,
With feet that make no sound upon the floors.

Completed in 1917, the Dudley Coe Health Center filled a long-standing need for an infirmary on the Bowdoin campus. Thomas Upham Cole, of the class of 1857, himself a man of medicine, undertook the entirety of expense for the construction and asked in return only that the building be named in honor of his son Dudley, who had died as a young boy. A portrait of the boy as a toddler hung for many years in the front parlor of the building, and even though young Dudley had died long before a brick was ever laid for his building, the inhabitants of the health center saw that portrait and began to ascribe the strange incidents they witnessed to the spirit of young Dudley. The portrait shows the observer an angelic face, to be sure, but there is perhaps in his expression just a hint of playfulness as well. So when a door suddenly slammed shut on its own accord, the staff would just nod and say, "There goes Dudley!'"

No one has ever accused Dudley of being malicious. As spirits go, he is much more of a practical joker. Besides slamming doors to startle people, Dudley liked to turn radios on for people, and for some reason, Dudley amused himself by flushing the toilets. The medical staff had become so accustomed to the prankish flushing that they didn't even notice it happening one day when contractors were replacing them. The men came down to the nurses' station to report that the toilets were flushing themselves. The nurses

Dudley Coe Health Center. *Author's collection.*

said, "Oh, that's just Dudley," but the repairmen went on to explain that the toilets flushing themselves hadn't even been hooked up yet.

"Dudley isn't a scary ghost at all," a former staff person stated. "He's very friendly. We're used to him, and I think we'd miss him if he wasn't there!"

Even so, his little pranks can be unnerving. Leslie Nuccio is an insurance coordinator for Health Services who had worked in the building for five years and was used to Dudley's activities. One time, while she was alone in the building, she had gone to the second-floor bathroom. As she was drying her hands, she happened to look up at the mirror above the sink. She said, "Just as if someone was behind me, splashing water with their hands, there was water all over the mirror! Needless to say, I cut that day short and went home. I was too spooked to stay there alone!"

In 2009, the health center moved into the new Peter Buck Center for Health and Fitness, and the Dudley Coe is now used mostly as offices for the college's Upward Bound program, counseling services and the Isle Program. I have not heard that anyone working among them has experienced any of Dudley's antics. Nuccio muses about what Dudley does now: "I'm rather happy to be in our new place, especially when I'm alone working here in the summer, [but] we often wonder if our ghost there misses us!"

Chapter 16

CHAMBER OF HORRORS

O'er whose unsteady floor, that sways and bends,
Wander our thoughts above the dark abyss.

At the time of Bowdoin College's formative years, the world was entering what Thomas Paine famously described as the "Age of Reason." In New England, in particular, having long been fashioned and guided by the strict and somber principles of Puritanism, this popularization of reexamining long-held truths no doubt helped the fledgling institution attract inquiring minds. Curiously, this freedom to interpret universal truths also brought about a revitalization of spiritualism as people began to question millennia-old doctrines. Like Paine himself, many people did not abandon religion for reason but began to question its foundations and mantras. Shakers, Mormons and a new wave of separatist "utopian" communities all sprang up at this time. In literature and philosophy, we see the appearance of the transcendentalists of Ralph Waldo Emerson and Henry Thoreau, who borrowed freely from Hindu texts in a manner that would almost certainly have had them hanged or banished but three hundred years earlier. As a junior pastor in Boston in 1832, Emerson gave voice in his diary to beginnings of these once unheard of queries: "I have sometimes thought that, in order to be a good minister, it was necessary to leave the ministry. The profession is antiquated. In an altered age, we worship in the dead forms of our forefathers."

With newfound freedom for exploration, there also arose a fascination with the occult and secret societies. Secret societies such as Free Masons and various forms of Rosicrucianism had existed throughout the world for centuries, typically combining the basic tenets of Christianity with the rites and metaphysics not tolerated in the established Western churches. Groups like the Oneida Community and Mormons felt emboldened enough to pursue new beliefs, while others felt comfortable enough to dabble in or at least ponder mysteries and rites without certain knowledge of their eternal damnation. At colleges and universities in the burgeoning republic, the rise of these secret societies was understandably interesting to the minds of imaginative young men getting their first real experience of independent life. Famous secret societies such as Yale University's still powerful Skull and Bones came into existence at this time.

At Bowdoin College, the appearance of secret societies, first springing up in the 1840s, was met with mixed reactions. The arguments for each side are echoed today in the ongoing debates about college fraternities and sororities, which are the descendants of these original societies. Many

The Tomb, home of Yale's Skull and Bones. *Library of Congress, Prints and Photographs Division (Wikipedia).*

faculty and students argued that the societies were healthy endeavors for Bowdoin gentlemen that promoted philanthropy, intellectualism and the bonds of brotherhood. Others argued there was a primal flaw in any organization that felt it had to be exclusive and secretive. "They foster a spirit of clannishness," wrote President Ezekiel Gilman Robinson of Brown University. "They intensify peculiarities of taste and habit, till these harden into defects of character." Stories of improprieties began to surface about the goings-on at some of these secret meetings. An article in the May 26, 1880 edition of the *Bowdoin Orient* reports that "the Faculty also, after a few years, conceived a dislike for the societies and resolved to abolish them," but after but a few years of existence, the societies were so entrenched that the students could confidently tell the faculty to "go to—heaven." Nevertheless, the merit of these secret societies was still hotly debated, as a perusal of the student newspaper the *Bowdoin Orient* during this time shows.

In the summer of 1897, during renovations to Bowdoin's Appleton Hall, the naysayers to secret societies benefited from a disturbing discovery that made national headlines. The *Philadelphia Evening Telegraph* mentions the incident in a short article on July 20 titled "A Dungeon under Bowdoin College." In the article, it was revealed that workmen toiling on the foundations of Appleton were horrified to find there "an array of skulls and skeletons, arranged in fantastic disorder." The article went on to report that passageways leading up from the hidden vault opened up into secret entrances in students' rooms.

The story caught fire, and more articles about the discovery appeared in Boston, Chicago, Philadelphia and St. Louis. The following are some headlines and choice quotes from articles that appeared in various newspaper across the country as a result of the 1897 discovery under Appleton Hall:

A DUNGEON UNDER BOWDOIN COLLEGE.
The Cavern Uncovered by Workmen Contained Skeletons—A Hazing Inferno?
…there was an array of skulls and skeletons arranged in fantastic disorder. Some coffins lent their dismal presence to the atmosphere of death. The workmen scampered out of this underground place with their eyes staring and could not be induced to venture back.
—Philadelphia Evening Telegraph, *July 20*

The Chi Psi symbols on the doorway of Reed House with a skull and crossbones. *Holly Sherburne.*

FOUND A COLLEGE DUNGEON.
The Astonishing Cavern Some Workmen at Bowdoin Discovered While Digging.
…The walls were lined with somber black, so that the darkness was inky.
—New York Sun, *July 20*

COLLEGE MYSTERY REVEALED. Cavern Full of Grinning Skulls
Unearthed at Bowdoin
—Springfield Union News, *July 21*

CAVE OF SKELETONS. Gruesome Spot Used Probably by Bowdoin Students.
…Workmen recently blundered across it and were horrified to find there a
fantastic array of skeletons, coffins, and skulls…
—Wilmington Morning News, *July 21*

The place had a varied assortment of coffins, skulls, crossbones and other ghastly paraphernalia. The walls were painted a deep black color, and the general aspect of the chamber was revolting and horrible. Was it one of a long series of catacombs where recalcitrant sinners or heretics were slain and buried?
—Boston Republican, *July 31*

At one end of the building was found a dungeon cell or cave, fitted up in the most terrifying manner. Its walls were lined with black, no light could penetrate it, and in this vault was a grotesque array of skulls and skeletons, and strangest of all, a coffin.
—New York Evening Post, *August 10*

…curious discovery is reported from Bowdoin college, Maine. In excavating for the remodeling of Appleton hall, one of the college dormitories, the laborers came across a subterranean chamber beneath the cellar of the structure. The chamber had evidently been untouched for years, was draped in black and contained some skeletons and coffins. Further investigations proved that the chamber was connected with some of the students' dormitories…
—Chicago Chronicle, *August 1*

No doubt the most shocking was the front-page article run by the *New York Evening Post* on July 24 of that year. The headline read "Chamber of Horrors Found Under a Dormitory at Bowdoin College." The front-page story asked the reader to imagine the torture a hazing candidate was subjected to, being placed inside the coffin and lowered into the cave by the fraternity's members and left to lie alone and helpless in that subterranean nightmare until his torturers had deemed he had suffered enough. Included with the article was a large and imaginative illustration of what the chamber must have been like and what sort of rituals its occupants must have enjoyed during its heyday. Grinning, maniacal members hold skulls aloft while an unfortunate blindfolded victim is persecuted with some strange apparatus.

The *New York Evening Post* article also calls the reader's attention to the fact that Bowdoin College had many illustrious alumni who probably knew about this chamber and the activities going on down there. Indeed, the article states that "many prominent men [were] implicated in its dark deeds." Thomas Brackett Reed (class of 1860), the representative from Maine, was mentioned, as was Chief Justice Melville Fuller (class of 1853), along with

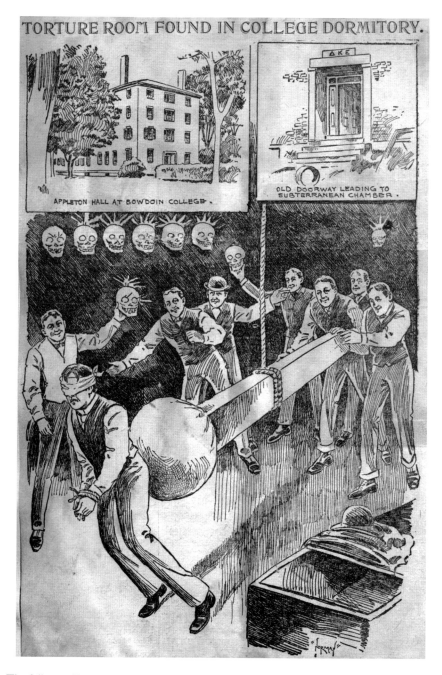

The full-page illustration of the envisioned "Chamber of Horrors" that ran in the *New York Evening Post* in 1897. *Documentary History Scrapbook, 1896–1897, Office of Communications and Public Affairs: publications, news releases, records, George J. Mitchell Dept. of Special Collections & Archives. Bowdoin College Library. Brunswick, Maine.*

judges, bishops, generals and senators. "Opinion is greatly divided," the *Post* notes, "as to the dark deeds which have been transacted in this gloomy cell."

Fears of men in power forming allegiances with secret societies were prominent in nineteenth-century America. The Anti-Masonic Party formed in 1828 around concerns that Freemasonry was corrupting the ideals of the republic with its secrecy and elitism, with many members holding the belief that Freemasons were murdering those who spoke out against their reign. Although the party waned and was subsumed by the Whig Party, as late as 1884, an Anti-Masonic Party put up a candidate for president who stood for the abolition of all secret societies.

Despite the flurry of articles and escalation of rhetoric about this "Chamber of Horrors," the story quickly faded from the public attention. It seems likely that the original details reported about the find were greatly overstated. As an article in the *New York Tribune* stated on August 2:

> *A good deal of interest seems to have been aroused in the reported discovery of an underground chamber in one of the buildings of Bowdoin College. The facts of the case are as follows…In the course of their tearing down and overhauling the workmen found, in one of the large archways beneath one of the big chimneys, an old coffin, a log, and a few other articles. There was no "room" or "dungeon" or anything of that sort—only this archway and an open but unused cellar.*

The true details of what was unearthed under Appleton Hall in the summer of 1897 will probably never be known for sure, but there is at least one remnant of Bowdoin's history still in existence that harkens back to these days. Located just off the main campus stands what is today called Reed House, after the aforementioned Thomas Brackett Reed, but was previously the home of the Alpha Eta of Chi Psi fraternity. This house, now a dormitory for around thirty Bowdoin students, does in fact possess a sub-chamber in its basement and was unquestionably used by the fraternity. In the basement of the building is a heavily padlocked wooden door, and beyond that is a set of stairs that lead you farther down to a set of rarely seen rooms. Passing through another ancient and dilapidated wooden door, you enter into a chamber that was clearly at one point quite impressive. Wires dangle uselessly from the ceiling where once ornate chandeliers hung. Along each wall are stationed benches where members would gather for meetings. At the front of the room is a great dais where issues were debated and judgments were passed. And sitting in the middle of the room, atop a great

The subterranean meeting hall of the Chi Psi brothers, complete with hazing coffin. *Holly Sherburne.*

stone wheel that was once surrounded by candles, there remains a coffin where pledges were put through whatever rigors were deemed necessary by the brothers.

The room has been sealed since the building stopped being a fraternity, but it remains much as it was and continues as a reminder of secret societies and their debatable influence of college society.

Chapter 17

HERE LIES ANNA

The spirit-world around this world of sense

Every day, students and faculty traipse the busy walkway between Appleton and Hyde Halls, never suspecting that they are passing right in front of three hidden graves. To be sure, the graves are easy to miss, as they are tucked neatly into the gardens that lie just outside the south entrance to Appleton. The most distinct of the graves barely juts more than four inches above the turf, and when the gardens are in bloom, the graves are fully obscured. Even in the early spring or late autumn, one could easily mistake the simple stones for edging. But if you take the trouble to bend down and clear away any branches, you will see a memorial with distinct embossed lettering: "ANNA '78." Take a few steps eastward, and you will realize this stone isn't alone. Similar, more rudimentary graves marked "ANNA '80" and "ANNA '00" also adorn the garden.

Who was Anna? Well, as it turns out, "Anna" is the first name of Anna Lytica. These stones are all that remain to be found of a curious custom that was at one time popular at Bowdoin and other colleges around the country. Upon completing some rigorous course in a particular field, students would take it upon themselves to hold funerals for their textbooks. In this case, Anna Lytica was their personification of analytical geometry.

Students frequently made a lavish production of these funerals. Louis Clinton Hatch, in his definitive *History of Bowdoin College,* tells us that in 1859, the "mourners" came out in their finest clothes, painstakingly cleaned, to

Left: An Anna "tombstone" from the class of 1878. *Holly Sherburne.*

Below: Program from the class of 1876's funeral for Anna. *From* Class of 1876 *(Bowdoin College yearbook).*

ORDO EXERCITATIONUM.

Cantus a Caterva Musicorum.

LAUDATIO - - - - - - - GUILIELMUS G. WAITT.

Cantus a Caterva Musicorum.

ELEGIA - - - - - - - - - ARLO BATES.

Carmen a Cantoribus.

PROFECTIO AD PYRAM.

$$[\text{in forma } y-y' = \frac{y''-y'}{x''-x''}(x-x')]$$

Carmen Lugubre.

LAMENTATIO - - - - - - OLIVERUS C. STEVENS.

Carmen a Cantoribus.

Crematio.

Carmen a Classe.

Luctuosus Tumultus.

"WARUP."

attend the ceremony. An immense funeral pyre, formed of the students' textbooks, was then set ablaze. Traditionally, the ashes would be collected and buried in a coffin, and "a stone with a suitable inscription was placed at the grave." In 1875, the college newspaper the *Orient* reported that the funeral rites for a textbook included an official eulogist and that an elegy was also written for the occasion. Both were received with "groans and sobs" from the bereaved. Programs written in Latin were printed to mark the solemnity of the occasion as well.

This ritual was a common enough tradition that other little graves probably exist throughout the campus, but time, nature and development has hidden them forever from view. Even these stones would not have been saved if not for the intervention of some Bowdoin faculty who knew the history behind them. Several years back, a construction project was undertaken by the college to reconfigure the walkways behind Massachusetts Hall. Dale Syphers, a professor of physics at Bowdoin who knew there were textbook graves in the place they were working, asked them if they had taken up the gravestones. The response of the project manager was one of immediate concern and horror: "Are you telling me there are *people* buried there?" Syphers explained the history, and the stones were discovered among the piles of earth they had already moved. Doing their best to avoid any further desecration (without completely interfering with the construction), the three stones were relocated to their current position outside Appleton Hall. Another stone was moved only a short distance, and "ANNA '77" can be found in a small patch of grass between walkways on the eastern side of Massachusetts Hall. The actual earthly remains of the dear departed Annas, of course, could not be found.

Professor Syphers and students presiding over MOM's final ceremony. *Dale Syphers.*

HUMATIO MOM

NEPTIS CARE ANNÆ LYTICÆ

— IN —

COLLEGIO BOWDOINENSI,

Mense Decembris,

MMXIII,

— AB —

PHYS2220,

CELEBRABITUR.

Corpus MOM mortuæ secunda noctis vigilia
in statu in loco Physico jacet;
unde in humeros vespilionum
ad veterem Pinum feretur.

Left: The 2013 program for MOM's funeral, complete with traditional Latin text. *Dale Syphers.*

Below: MOM's headstone. *Dale Syphers.*

Interestingly, in 2013, Professor Syphers revived this unique tradition. His Engineering Physics class held a burial ceremony for the course textbook *Mechanics of Materials*. The class referred to this tome as "beloved granddaughter of Anna." The funeral ceremony included the traditional Latin program, and a granite gravestone was commissioned. But the gravestone for this textbook could not be given the traditional name of

Anna. Instead, the class just shortened *Mechanics of Materials* and simply chiseled in: "MOM."

For those readers disappointed in not discovering true human remains buried on campus, you can always venture just off campus proper and into the beautiful pine groves that buffer Whittier field from Harpswell Road. There, if you leave the main trails you can find a plaque as often overlooked as the gravestones in front of Appleton Hall. You will find it fastened to a great tree, and it reads:

> *BENEATH THESE PINES*
> *ARE SPREAD THE ASHES OF*
> *ROLAND EUGENE CLARK*
> *BOWDOIN 1901*
> *TREASURER OF THE COLLEGE*
> *1949–1959*

Plaque in the Bowdoin Pines that marks the location of Roland Eugene Clark's remains. This is the closest one comes to a real grave site on the campus. *Author's collection.*

Chapter 18

GHOSTS AND GENERALS

Impalpable impressions on the air

Located just on the other side of Maine Street from the Bowdoin College
campus sits the Joshua Lawrence Chamberlain Museum. Saved from
demolition when it was purchased by the Pejepscot Historical Society in
1983, the building has a long connection with its collegiate neighbor.

When it was built around 1824, it actually resided farther westward
at number 4 Potter Street. At one point in the 1830s, Henry Wadsworth
Longfellow, then a professor of modern languages at Bowdoin College,
rented three rooms in the house. The house was sold a number of times
and was finally purchased in 1859 by Joshua Lawrence Chamberlain, who
had returned to teach at Bowdoin after graduating in 1852. After the Civil
War, Chamberlain sold a portion of his home's original plot and had the
house moved to its current location. Chamberlain lived there until his
death in 1914.

Today, the museum serves as a reminder and tribute to one of Bowdoin's
most famous alumni. Although always well known in Maine history,
Chamberlain's fame reached new levels with Michael Shaara's 1975 Pulitzer
Prize–winning novel *The Killer Angels*, which presents the days leading up
to the Battle of Gettysburg from the perspectives of many of the leading
protagonists, including a young Colonel Chamberlain. Shaara's coverage of
Chamberlain and his famous downhill bayonet charge on Little Round Top
have made Chamberlain a popular figure among Civil War enthusiasts, with

The Joshua Lawrence Chamberlain Museum. Notice the chimney with the Twentieth Maine emblem and the second-floor balcony door that was the front door before the first floor became the second floor. *Reroche (Wikipedia).*

the Twentieth Maine Monument at Gettysburg becoming the favorite site at the national park.

One story that Shaara doesn't put in his novel is a legend of spectral assistance received by the Twentieth Maine during that Gettysburg venture. Chamberlain himself makes mention of a part of the story in his book *Through Blood & Fire at Gettysburg,* and the legend has grown in the continued telling. Simply put, the legend states that the ghost of George Washington himself intervened in the hours before the battle, as well as during its most furious moments of bloodshed. Chamberlain writes, "Now from a dark angle of the roadside came a whisper, whether from earthly or unearthly voice one cannot feel quite sure, that the august form of Washington had been seen that afternoon at sunset riding over the Gettysburg hills. Let no one smile at me! I half believed it myself—so did the powers of the other world draw nigh!"

If the revered founding father was to take a hand in the battle, it wouldn't be a complete surprise that he should appear to troops under

Chamberlain's command. After all, Chamberlain's great-grandfather Franklin Chamberlain had been a soldier at Yorktown in the American Revolutionary War, the ultimate victory for General George Washington and his Continental army.

In her book *Civil War Ghost Stories & Legends,* Nancy Roberts included more details, claiming that Washington even appeared at a crossroads and directed the Twentieth Maine on the right path so the soldiers would not be late for the battle and their moment of destiny. Later, on Little Round Top after Chamberlain made his famous cry, "Bayonet! Forward!" Roberts reports that Union soldiers saw Washington again. She said, "Suddenly, an imposing figure stood in front of the line exhorting them to follow. The rays of the afternoon sun set his upraised sword aflame. Once more the Twentieth Maine was seized by the same exultation they had felt following the phantom horseman on the road to Little Round Top. *He* was leading them again!"

Reports of the phantasm that led the charge down Little Round Top continued to be told after the war had ended. Even Confederate soldiers reported that bullets fired at the figure simply passed through without harming him. Roberts concludes her tale with an interview Chamberlain gave many years later in which he was questioned about the George Washington legend. Chamberlain responded:

> *Yes, that report was circulated through our lines, and I have no doubt that it had a tremendous psychological effect in inspiring the men. Doubtless it was a superstition, but who among us can say that such a thing was impossible...*
>
> *We know not what mystic power may be possessed by those who are now bivouacking with the dead. I only know the effect, but I dare not explain or deny the cause. I do believe that we were enveloped by the powers of the other world that day and who shall say that Washington was not among the number of those who aided the country that he founded?*

Washington's specter may have been impervious to bullets that day, but Chamberlain would go on to often feel the searing effects of hot lead. He was wounded six times, had six horses shot out from under him and, at the Siege of Petersburg, received a shot through his hips that was so devastating he wasn't expected to survive. Instead of falling, Chamberlain drew out his sword and stuck it into the ground so he could lean on it for support. From this position, he encouraged his men to continue the attack until he finally lost consciousness from loss of blood.

When the Civil War ended, Chamberlain returned to his home on Potter Street, moving it a few years later, as previously stated, to its current location. Chamberlain rode his wartime popularity to four single-year terms as governor of Maine and in 1871 became president of Bowdoin College. Curiously, he didn't move into 85 Federal, as presidents before him had done, but instead renovated his little Cape, raising the building eleven feet off the ground and having a new "first floor" built beneath it that was large enough to welcome visitors in a fashion deemed fitting for a college president.

After his death in 1914, the Chamberlain House remained connected to the college but mostly as a rental property for students. Chamberlain's granddaughter sold the house to Emery Brooker in 1939, and up until it was purchased by the Pejepscot Historical Society, it served as a seven-unit apartment house.

Today, the house serves as a valuable resource for Chamberlain aficionados in Brunswick and beyond. And not surprisingly, reports of apparitions and other paranormal experiences have been described in this almost two-hundred-year-old edifice. People have claimed to have seen the ghosts of Chamberlain and his wife, Fanny, at different times when visiting the house. Other people have said that when visiting, they are suddenly afflicted with a sharp pain in their hips, much like that Chamberlain suffered at Petersburg.

Chapter 19

I KNOW WHERE THE BODIES ARE BURIED

From graves forgotten stretch their dusty hands,
And hold in mortmain still their old estates.

"Oh, Coleman Hall is *definitely* haunted," a student resolutely stated on one of my most recent tours as we approached the brick dormitory. "Do you know the story about Coleman?" I asked her. "No, but it has so many weird noises and things happening in it, I just know it must be," she replied. When I took a group of school administrators on the tour one time, they had to agree that Coleman Hall had a reputation for being the hardest residence hall for students and that it produced more cases of medical leave than any other dormitory per capita.

If these reports bear out, then maybe there is some truth to the long-held belief among the residents of Coleman Hall that their building holds a dark and sinister history that predates the construction of the building itself.

To appreciate the legend, we must turn our attention back to Adams Hall and the Medical School of Maine. The medical school received strong funding in its early years and produced over two thousand graduates during its one-hundred-year existence. An article in the *Bowdoin Orient* in 1880 states, "We can predict nothing but success in its future," but by the dawn of the twentieth century, the college simply did not possess the resources to maintain a modern clinical environment. Following a particularly scathing report on the condition of its curriculum, the trustees decided in 1921 to close the school for good.

Coleman Hall. *Author's collection.*

Should they really be digging here? Groundbreaking ceremonies for Coleman Hall in 1958. *Bowdoin College Archives, Brunswick, Maine.*

That was the end of the Medical School of Maine, but what happened to all of the school's inventory? In particular, what did it decide to do with the research cadavers it had on hand but no longer had any use for? There were certainly no medical waste companies to handle the school's needs, and the corpses, if they could be identified at all, were typically paupers or convicted criminals—not the kind of people local townspeople wanted interred in their otherwise respectable graveyards. At any rate, the local undertaker would be sure to charge a fee for each burial and plot. And so, the story among Coleman occupants goes, in the dark of night, the administration arranged for the leftover bodies to be taken from the basement of Adams Hall, carted to the unused grassy lot at the edge of College Street and hastily buried. Years later, all memory of the act was forgotten, and in 1958, Bowdoin innocently built Coleman Hall on that open lawn.

Now, it should be stated that there is no historical evidence to corroborate this tale told by Coleman residents, but then again, there are no official reports about what *did* happen to all those corpses either. And there must be some explanation for all those disturbances reported in Coleman Hall today!

Chapter 20

THE DEAD SHIP OF HARPSWELL

And as the moon from some dark gate of cloud
Throws o'er the sea a floating bridge of light

Just catty-corner to Coleman Hall on the other side of College Street is another vacant grassy lot. The property is bordered by lines of young arborvitae trees and is surrounded by college buildings, a private residence and the Coffin Street parking lot. Bowdoin College has owned the space since 2007, but prior to that, the lot held the home and birthplace of Robert P.T. Coffin, of the class of 1915. When the college purchased the property, it offered the home for free to anyone willing to move it and preserve the landmark, but the building was so dilapidated at that point that no takers could be found, and the house was demolished.

Coffin was a native of Brunswick, and the Coffin family was deeply entrenched in New England history, with the first Coffins arriving in America as far back as 1642. After attending Bowdoin, Robert P.T. Coffin earned degrees from Princeton and Oxford, eventually returning to Bowdoin as a professor and winning a Pulitzer Prize for poetry in 1936. Coffin wrote a great deal about local New England topics and legends, including his most famous work, *Captain Abby and Captain John*, which is set in the once rich and prominent shipbuilding district of Brunswick known as Pennellville.

Another of Coffin's books builds on a popular legend of Harpswell, Maine, known as the Dead Ship of Harpswell or the Ghost Ship of Harpswell. In his book *John Dawn*, the title character encounters the ghostly ship once when he is young, just before his father dies, and again shortly before his own death. This is in accordance with the actual legend of the ghost ship that it is spotted as a premonition of death for oneself or family members.

This famous ghost ship was originally christened the *Dash*. Built in 1812 in the yards of Freeport, Maine, it was built as a blockade runner against the English navy, but the *Dash* soon proved formidable as an American privateer, predating on English merchant ships and engaging or evading the powerful English frigates. It became famous for its successful attacks and daring escapes, and every Maine sailor wanted to sail aboard the *Dash*.

The *Dash* made what people thought was its final voyage in 1815. Heading out of Portland, it encountered a powerful winter storm and vanished. No report of wreckage ever came to shore, but people assumed the ship was lost and all hands gone for good.

It wasn't until family members of the *Dash*'s crew in Harpswell began to pass away that people started thinking about the ship again. On the night that the brother of a crew member had died, several people reported seeing the *Dash* sailing in the harbor. As Rose O'Brien wrote in her article about the legend in the *Lewiston Sun Journal* in 1955: "It came in quietly, and it never landed. It never even made a tiny ripple on the water. It just came in and was there and then it was gone. And when it sailed out, the kinsman was dead."

As years passed, more relatives of the *Dash*'s crew passed away, and with each death, there came a sighting of the phantom ship. People believed that the ship was coming to take their loved ones' souls on to eternal rest.

Even after all the family members of the long-departed crew of the *Dash* had died, the legend of the Dead Ship of Harpswell could not be stopped. A fisherman was plying his trade in Casco Bay when a thick fog suddenly rolled in. Through the mists, the man saw a full-rigged sailing ship heading toward him. The fisherman was frightened because the sails were full and blowing, but there was absolutely no wind in the air to move the fog, let alone a great sailing ship. As the ship passed him by, he saw the name on the prow: "*Dash*—Freeport."

Reports of the *Dash* kept coming in from fishermen who would encounter it in a still fog. "She flew past me like a whirlwind," tells Roscoe Moulton in *Historic Haunted America*. "And they warn't a breath of air stirring." The entire crew of the cod fisher the *Betty Macomber* reported seeing the *Dash* speed in front of them on their way into shore, and this time they even reported seeing the original crew on the old schooner's decks.

Perhaps the most interesting story in modern times involves the *Dash* playing "catch me if you can" with a number of navy boats. During World

War II, ships from both the U.S. Navy and the British Royal Navy frequently patrolled the waters of Casco Bay. On a foggy day in August 1942, Homer Grimm had rowed his small boat over to Wolfe's Neck from his home on Staple's Point. Once on shore, he was startled to hear a great to-do as alarm sirens went off from the patrolling destroyers. The modern navy vessels appeared cutting through the mists of Cumberland Cove, clearly in pursuit of something that must have appeared on their new radar screens. Scanning to the other direction, Grimm looked to see if he could get a glimpse of their target. Through a brief rent in the vapors, there suddenly appeared a great old-time masted schooner, peopled with sailors in old-fashioned sea garb. Before the clouds swept back in, he read on the name on the stern.

It was the *Dash*.

The legend of the ghost ship continues to this day with occasional sightings reported. In a 2012 online article in the *Progressive Review*, Sam Smith, a Harpswell native, recalled an incident in 1975 when he was eating lunch with his mother overlooking the Casco Bay. His mother looked up suddenly and said, "Oh look, there goes the ghost ship of Harpswell." Smith thought she was just making a joke, but later that day, his father was discovered down

A topsail schooner like the *Dash* of Freeport, which came to be known as the Dead Ship of Harpswell. *Thomas Butterworth (Wikipedia).*

by the shore, dead of a heart attack. The ghost ship was still collecting the souls of departing family members, it seems.

John Greenleaf Whittier, the famed nineteenth-century New England poet, published a poem in the June 1866 edition of the *Atlantic Monthly* that perhaps best captures the essence of this long-cherished piece of Harpswell folklore. The "Dead Ship of Harpswell" is an eerie bit of verse, but it also contains a message of cheer and encouragement for those coastal families who are visited by the spectral vessel:

> *WHAT flecks the outer gray beyond*
> *The sundown's golden trail?*
> *The white flash of a sea-bird's wing,*
> *Or gleam of slanting sail?*
> *Let young eyes watch from Neck and Point,*
> *And sea-worn elders pray,—*
> *The ghost of what was once a ship*
> *Is sailing up the bay!*
>
> *From gray sea-fog, from icy drift,*
> *From peril and from pain,*
> *The home-bound fisher greets thy lights,*
> *O hundred-harbored Maine!*
> *But many a keel shall seaward turn,*
> *And many a sail outstand,*
> *When, tall and white, the Dead Ship looms*
> *Against the dusk of land.*
>
> *She rounds the headland's bristling pines;*
> *She threads the isle-set bay;*
> *No spur of breeze can speed her on,*
> *Nor ebb of tide delay.*
> *Old men still walk the Isle of Orr*
> *Who tell her date and name,*
> *Old shipwrights sit in Freeport yards*
> *Who hewed her oaken frame.*
>
> *What weary doom of baffled quest,*
> *Thou sad sea-ghost, is thine?*
> *What makes thee in the haunts of home*

A wonder and a sign?
No foot is on thy silent deck,
Upon thy helm no hand;
No ripple hath the soundless wind
That smites thee from the land!

For never comes the ship to port,
Howe'er the breeze may be;
Just when she nears the waiting shore
She drifts again to sea.
No tack of sail, nor turn of helm,
Nor sheer of veering side;
Stern-fore she drives to sea and night,
Against the wind and tide.

In vain o'er Harpswell Neck the star
Of evening guides her in;
In vain for her the lamps are lit
Within thy tower, Seguin!
In vain the harbor-boat shall hail,
In vain the pilot call;
No hand shall reef her spectral sail,
Or let her anchor fall.

Shake, brown old wives, with dreary joy,
Your gray-head hints of ill;
And, over sick-beds whispering low,
Your prophecies fulfil.
Some home amid yon birchen trees
Shall drape its door with woe;
And slowly where the Dead Ship sails,
The burial boat shall row!

From Wolf Neck and from Flying Point,
From island and from main,
From sheltered cove and tided creek,
Shall glide the funeral train.
The dead-boat with the bearers four,
The mourners at her stern,—

And one shall go the silent way
Who shall no more return!

And men shall sigh, and women weep,
Whose dear ones pale and pine,
And sadly over sunset seas
Await the ghostly sign.
They know not that its sails are filled
By pity's tender breath,
Nor see the Angel at the helm
Who steers the Ship of Death!

Taking the Tour

This appendix is a rendering of this book in the form of the tour I typically give. If you have the opportunity to visit the Bowdoin College campus, you may find this a practical tour route for a self-guided experience. Each tour stop provides directions to the spot, geographic coordinates, accessibility and hours of availability at the time of publication. A brief summary of the tour spot is provided to give the reader a sense of what to expect, but for full details, references back to the appropriate chapter in the book are provided in each case.

Thorne Hall Basement

Full text: Chapter 2. Contains photo of basement.
Access and availability: Typically not accessible to the public.
Approximate geo-coordinates: 43.905604, -69.963250
Directions: The Coles Tower complex, including Thorne Hall, is located on the south end of the Bowdoin College campus. Coles Tower is the highest building on campus. From the main campus, cross College Street and walk toward Coles. At the end of the sidewalk, bear left toward Sarah Orne Jewett Hall. If you stand by the loading dock between Thorne and Jewett Halls, you will be standing just about exactly over the basement.
What to see: The upstairs dining area and stairwell leading to the basement.
Summary: The basement of Thorne Hall has long been a source of rumor and unease among the dining staff at Bowdoin. No one likes to go down to

the cellar at night alone. Lights in the hallway frequently switch themselves on and off, and the elevator doors at the far end open and close on their own accord. Everyone who visits the building complains about feeling watched and unwelcome. Several employees have reported hearing voices when down there on their own.

John Brown Russwurm African American Center

Full text: Chapter 3. Contains photo of building and photos of Alpheus Spring Packard and William Smyth.

Access and availability: Open most weekdays when classes are in session. However, there is no reception area, so be sensitive to college work and events when visiting.

Approximate geo-coordinates: 43.906676, -69.963497

Directions: From Coles Tower complex, walk northward toward College Street and the main campus. The John Brown Russwurm African American Center will be on your left, catty-corner to the Alpheus Spring Packard Gateway.

What to see: The building is the original Packard-Smyth House built in 1827 and from the outside looks quite similar to its original construction. The inside has been drastically renovated over the years but still demonstrates some of the home's original structure.

Summary: People have reported feeling a presence, which is sometimes accompanied by sudden temperature drops on hot summer evenings. A student saw the shadow of a human form appear on the far wall of the library and pass out of the room even though there was no one else around. Various people report odd tapping sounds that reverberate through the building at no particular time or season.

Hawthorne-Longfellow Library

Full text: Chapters 8 and 9. Includes images of Longfellow and Hawthorne and a scene from the Salem Witch trials.

Access and availability: Open 8:00 a.m. to 1:30 a.m. when classes are in session on weekdays and 10:00 a.m. to 11:00 p.m. on weekends. Open weekdays 8:00 a.m. to 5:00 p.m. in the summer.

Approximate geo-coordinates: 43.907046, -69.963638

Directions: From the Russwurm Center, walk northward across College Street. The front doors of the Hawthorne-Longfellow Library will be directly on your left.

What to see: Oil paintings of Henry Wadsworth Longfellow and Nathaniel Hawthorne hang on opposite walls of the library's front entrance.

Summary: Both of Bowdoin's most famous alumni, Henry Wadsworth Longfellow and Nathaniel Hawthorne, have a number of interesting connections to paranormal stories both in history and literature.

Hubbard Stacks

Full text: Chapter 7. Contains photos of stacks exterior and the translucent floors/ceilings.

Access and availability: Open 8:00 a.m. to 1:30 a.m. when classes are in session on weekdays and 10:00 a.m. to 11:00 p.m. on weekends. Open weekdays 8:00 a.m. to 5:00 p.m. in the summer. Alternatively, you can get an exterior view the stacks from the back and east side of Hubbard Hall.

Approximate geo-coordinates: 43.907298, -69.963187

Directions: To enter the stacks, continue from the library entrance and walk past the circulation desk. Turn left and take the door to the basement. Walk through the glass doors and follow the signs to the Hubbard Stacks. Alternatively, to simply view the stacks from outside, walk out from the front entrance and veer to the left toward Hubbard Hall. Following the sidewalk, the six floors of the stacks will be on your left.

What to see: The mysterious elevators, the translucent floors and ceilings and the overall general spookiness of the lonely stacks.

Summary: Security Officers at Bowdoin College recount an odd experience with the elevators in the old library stacks.

Hubbard Hall

Full Text: Chapters 4 and 5. Contains photos of the gargoyle, Hubbard's suite and various interior views.

Access and availability: Open during the day and early evening when classes are in session on weekdays and most weekends. Typically open until 5:00 p.m. during the summer.

Approximate geo-coordinates: 43.907693, -69.963154

Directions: From the front entrance of the library, walk out from the doors and veer to the left toward Hubbard Hall. Follow the sidewalk around the east side of the building, and turn left to approach the entrance of Hubbard Hall.

What to see: The Hubbard gargoyle, dangerous steps, various spots with ghost sightings and unexplained experiences and the President Edwards portrait.

Summary: Hubbard Hall is one of Bowdoin College's spookiest places on campus. It has some interesting history and several unexplained events, including strange whispers, objects moving on their own and one spectral appearance. The building has also had a number of unfortunate deaths associated it with it.

MEMORIAL FLAGPOLE

Full Text: Chapter 6. Contains a photo of the 1930 incident and the flagpole today.
Access and availability: Always available.
Approximate geo-coordinates: 43.907880, -69.963626
Directions: From the front entrance of Hubbard Hall, exit and turn left. Walk to the far corner of Hubbard Hall and take the sidewalk that veers to the right toward the Walker Art Museum. The flagpole is directly between Hubbard and the museum.
What to see: The flagpole and the chapel.
Summary: This tour stop focuses on famous college pranks. In particular, it tells the story of the Flagpole Incident, also referred to as the "Night of the Great Revolution," in which students in 1930 destroyed the works for a World War I memorial and moved the seventy-five-foot flagpole into the college chapel.

SEARLES SCIENCE BUILDING

Full text: Chapter 10. Contains photos of the building, the haunted hallway and Searles Castle.
Access and availability: Generally open weekdays and early evenings when class is in session. Open during the day in the summer.
Approximate geo-coordinates: 43.909364, -69.963071
Directions: From the Memorial Flagpole, walk northward past the Walker Art Museum and the Visual Arts Center. Searles Science Building is recognizable from its Gothic turrets and bell tower.
What to see: Gothic architecture. Hallway of the "echoing footsteps."
Summary: Outside of its general "noisiness," Searles Science Building has one particular noise that has disturbed its occupants for years. When walking through the long hallways, people report hearing footsteps behind them as though someone is right on their heels. When they turn around, no one is there. However, a few people have said they have seen a white, shadowy figure darting away out of the corner of their eyes. One legend

had it that the shadowy figure is the ghost of a girl who fell from one of the turrets when Searles was being built in 1894. More say that the apparition, and the heavy tread you can hear, belong to the spirit of a custodian who worked in the building for years.

Northwest Campus

Full text: Chapter 11. Contains photos of Curtis, Curtis's shack and an illustration of the college during Curtis's lifetime.
Access and availability: Always available.
Approximate geo-coordinates: 43.909743, -69.963157
Directions: From the Searles Science Building's front entrance, walk northward toward Memorial Hall. Stand somewhere between Searles and the newer addition to Memorial Hall.
What to see: Modern view of the edge of campus where "Diogenes" lived.
Summary: If you stand in the walkway between Pickard Theater and Searles Science Building and look toward the Joshua L. Chamberlain statue, you will be looking in the general direction of the spot where Thomas A. Curtis used to have a small shack just off the Bowdoin campus. Curtis arrived at Bowdoin in the summer of 1840 and became Bowdoin's personal handyman, running errands, mending clothes, cooking and cleaning. He also earned a bit of a reputation for being somewhat mad. Indeed, there was even a rumor that he had come to Brunswick to escape some dark secret past.

Joshua L. Chamberlain House

Full text: Chapter 18. Includes photo of the museum.
Access and availability: Open for tours May–October.
Approximate geo-coordinates: 43.910397, -69.963680
Directions: From the northwest of campus, follow the sidewalk westward through the college gates. The Chamberlain Museum is directly across the street from the Chamberlain statue.
What to see: Statue of Chamberlain and various items from Chamberlain's history in the museum.
Summary: Located just on the other side of Maine Street from the Bowdoin College campus sits the Joshua Lawrence Chamberlain Museum. The house was saved from demolition when it was purchased by the Pejepscot Historical Society in 1983. Joshua L. Chamberlain resided in the house as a professor and later as the president of Bowdoin College. People have claimed to have seen the ghosts of Chamberlain and his wife, Fanny,

at different times when visiting the house. Other people have said that when visiting, they are suddenly afflicted with a sharp pain in their hips like the pain that Chamberlain suffered when he was shot down at the Battle of Petersburg.

MASSACHUSETTS HALL

Full text: Chapter 12. Includes photos of Massachusetts Hall exterior and the seminar room.

Access and availability: Generally open weekdays and early evenings when class is in session. Open during the day in the summer. Be aware that when classes are in session, the seminar room may be in use.

Approximate geo-coordinates: 43.909581, -69.961981

Directions: From the Chamberlain Museum, cross back to campus. Walk through the campus gates and follow the sidewalk eastward past Memorial Hall. Massachusetts Hall is the next building on your left.

What to see: Seminar room, portrait of Joshua Chamberlain, door to restroom.

Summary: Massachusetts Hall was built in 1802, making it the oldest building on campus. Something in the building likes to play tricks on people. A story from a student studying alone there at night and another from a professor working late in the building provide two examples of the phenomenon.

ADAMS HALL

Full text: Chapter 13. Includes photos of the basement, coffin lid, cadaver hook and grisly medical school scenes.

Access and availability: Generally open weekdays and early evenings when class is in session. Open during the day in the summer. The basement is not accessible to the public.

Approximate geo-coordinates: 43.910000, -69.961127

Directions: Exiting from the front entrance of Massachusetts Hall, turn left and turn left again where the sidewalk tees. Walk on another 150 feet. Adams Hall is the first building on your right.

What to see: Winding staircase. Cadaver hook.

Summary: Adams Hall is generally seen as the centerpiece of the Bowdoin Haunted Tour. No other building has such a rich history of the paranormal—and is it any wonder? From 1861 until 1920, Adams Hall was the home of the Maine Medical School and, as such, had a steady stream of bodies being brought through its doors for dissection. Many of the bodies were shipped in from Maryland, where, at the time, grave robbing laws were lax. If you enter the basement of Adams Hall, you will go down to where the cadavers were kept "in pickle" until they were ready for use. You can still see the alcoves where the bodies were stored. The space in the center of the winding staircase was used for hoisting a cadaver-laden gurney up to the dissection rooms on the top floor. The hook used as a pulley remains on the top landing. Various disturbing stories from students and staff are recounted that include strange lights, apparitions and moving objects.

85 Federal Street

Full text: Chapter 14. Includes photos of 85 Federal exterior and Edith Sills entertaining guests.
Access and availability: Generally open weekdays, but keep in mind that 85 Federal is an office building and not a public space.
Approximate geo-coordinates: 43.910369, -69.959366
Directions: Exiting from the front entrance of Adams Hall, turn left and cross the campus road. Turn left again and follow the sidewalk to the college gates. Cross Bath Road and turn right. Follow the sidewalk until you reach Federal Street. The building at 85 Federal is recognizable by the prominent cupola on the roof.
What to see: Widow's walk. Building architecture.
Summary: 85 Federal was once the residence of President Kenneth Sills, and the staff members who work there have long said that his wife, Edith, still haunts the building. The first "sighting" came fifteen years after Edith died, when a secretary smelled Edith's perfume and felt a cold draft of air move through the hallway. Staff in next-door Cram Alumni House also report strange happenings.

Dudley Coe Building

Full text: Chapter 15. Includes a photo of the Dudley Coe Building.
Access and availability: Generally open weekdays, but keep in mind that Dudley Coe is an office building and not a public space.
Approximate geo-coordinates: 43.907657, -69.960454
Directions: From 85 Federal, retrace your steps back to Adams Hall and then walk into campus along Campus Drive. Walk past the chapel, then turn left and cross the grassy area behind the chapel and in between the two union buildings.

What to see: The first-floor restroom that Dudley plays in.

Summary: The Dudley Coe Building is named after the son of Thomas Upham Cole. Dudley died when he was fourteen, and many people believe his spirit haunts the building to this day. The large wooden doors in the building inexplicably slam shut, causing the staff to jump out of their seats and radios turn on and off by themselves. Most interestingly, Dudley amuses himself by flushing the toilets.

APPLETON HALL, NORTH SIDE

Full text: Chapter 16. Includes the *New York Evening Posts'* front-page article and a summary of various other clippings.

Access and availability: View of the doorway is always available. Appleton is inaccessible to the general public.

Approximate geo-coordinates: 43.908043, -69.962062

Directions: From Dudley Coe, retrace your step back toward the chapel. Locate the turnaround area of Campus Road. Appleton Hall is the rectangular brick building just beyond the turnaround area. The north end entrance will be on your right.

What to see: The entrance to the "chamber."

Summary: *Chamber of Horrors!* In 1897, during renovations to Appleton Hall, some Delta Kappa Epsilon relics were found in the basement. Several newspapers around the country reported that a torture chamber or dungeon had been found, including the *New York Evening Post*, which ran a sensational front-page story about the find on July 24 with the headline "Chamber of Horrors Found under a Dormitory at Bowdoin College!" Articles alleged that instruments of torture and human bones were among the finds.

APPLETON HALL, SOUTH SIDE

Full text: Chapter 17. Includes photos of stones and copies of the original funeral programs from the class of 1876.

Access and availability: Graves are always viewable, but be careful not to damage the flowers and plants.

Approximate geo-coordinates: 43.907681, -69.962236

Directions: From the north entrance of Appleton Hall, walk around the building on the quad side and position yourself by the doors on the other end.

What to see: The "Anna" stones.

Summary: Students and faculty take the walkway between Appleton and Hyde Halls everyday, but very few of them know that they are passing right by the grave of "Anna." Walk up to the door of Appleton and then look at the garden to your right, and you will see a gravestone marked "Anna," which stands for analytical geometry. In the 1800s, it was common practice on campus to have funerals for textbooks when the class was over. The funerals were often elaborate affairs with readings, bonfires and printed programs. Another such stone can be found outside Massachusetts Hall, and a new stone was placed outside Searles Science Building in 2014.

COLEMAN HALL

Full text: Chapter 19. Includes photos of modern Coleman Hall and the groundbreaking ceremony in 1957.
Access and availability: Coleman Hall is inaccessible to the general public.
Approximate geo-coordinates: 43.907161, -69.962656
Directions: Walking away from Appleton, bear left following the sidewalk that runs parallel to the road. Coleman Hall is the last building before College Street.
What to see: The exterior of Coleman Hall.
Summary: There is a legend among the residents of Coleman that when the medical school in Adams Hall closed its doors in 1920, the administrators of the college simply buried the remaining cadavers in the empty lot where Coleman stands today.

BIRTHPLACE OF ROBERT PETER TRISTRAM COFFIN

Full text: Chapter 20. Includes photo of a schooner like the *Dash* and the complete poem "The Dead Ship of Harpswell," by John Greenleaf Whittier.
Access and availability: Always accessible.
Approximate geo-coordinates: 43.906840, -69.961000
Directions: From Coleman Hall, walk to College Street and turn left. Take College Street until you reach Coffin Street. The site is on the far corner of College and Coffin.
What to see: The grassy spot where Coffin's house once stood.
Summary: Just off campus once stood the home of Robert Peter Tristram Coffin. Coffin liked to write Maine ghost stories, and in the book *John Dawn*, he writes about the Dead Ship of Harpswell, or the Ghost Ship of Harpswell, as it is commonly known. The ghost ship was a sailing ship that attacked British ships in the War of 1812. Christened the *Dash*, it vanished with all hands on a stormy night in 1815. Months later, fishermen would report

hearing a ship bear down on them in the fog and then see a phantom ship glide by with *Dash* inscribed on its bow. As the legend grew, people said that the ship appeared whenever a family member of one of the sixty original crew members died. The last reported sighting of the *Dash* was during World War II, when it appeared on a radar screen. When an intercept ship was sent in to investigate, it saw a ship called *Dash* vanish into the fog.

BIBLIOGRAPHY

Bangor Daily News. "Edith Sills Funeral Rites Set for Wednesday." August 29, 1978.

Baxtor, Percival C. "Editorial Notes." *Bowdoin Orient,* June 16, 1897.

Benét, Stephen Vincent. *The Devil and Daniel Webster and Other Writings.* New York: Penguin Classics, 1999.

Bowdoin Orient. "Athern P. Daggett: 1904–1973." February 2, 1973.

———. "Bowdoin's Hermit, Diogenes." March 31, 1886.

———. "Early History of Our Secret Societies." May 26, 1886.

———. "Photographer Strout Tells Tales of Old College Capers." May 16, 1934.

———. "Secret Societies." December 13, 1876.

Brown, Herbert Ross. *Sills of Bowdoin: The Life of Kenneth Charles Morton Sills, 1879–1954.* New York: Columbia University Press, 1964.

Calhoun, Charles C. *A Small College in Maine.* Brunswick, ME: Bowdoin College, 1993.

Chamberlain, Joshua Lawrence. *Through Blood & Fire at Gettysburg: General Joshua Chamberlain and the 20th Maine.* Gettysburg, PA: Stan Clark Military Books, 1994.

Citro, Joseph A. *Weird New England: Your Guide to New England's Best Kept Secrets.* New York: Sterling Publishing Co., 2005.

Coffin, Robert P. Tristram. *John Dawn.* New York: Macmillan Company, 1936.

Cross, John R. E-mail messages to author. April 2014.

———. "Night of the Great Revolution." *Bowdoin Daily Sun,* October 31, 2011. http://www.bowdoindailysun.com/2011/10/whispering-pines-night-of-the-great-revolution.

———. "Written in Stone." *Bowdoin Daily Sun,* September 21, 2010. http://www.bowdoindailysun.com/2010/09/whispering-pines-written-in-stone.

Dickey, Mark. Interview by author. Brunswick, Maine. October 13, 2005.

Documentary History Scrapbook, 1896–1897. Office of Communications and Public Affairs. George J. Mitchell Department of Special Collections and Archives. Bowdoin College Library. Brunswick, Maine.

Dustin-Hunter, Louann. E-mail message to author. October 13, 2005.

Emerson, Ralph Waldo. *Emerson in His Journals.* Edited by Joel Porte. Cambridge, MA: Belknap Press of Harvard University Press, 1982.

French, Timothy. Interview by author. Brunswick, Maine. September 2005.

Gutierez, Cathy. "Introduction." In *The Occult in Nineteenth-Century America.* Aurora, CO: Davies Group, 2005.

Hartford, Ernie. E-mail message to Chelsea Reid. October 27, 2008.

Hatch, Louis C. *History of Bowdoin College.* Portland, ME: Loring, Short & Harmon. 1927

Haunted Houses. "Longfellow's Wayside Inn." http://www.hauntedhouses.com/states/ma/longfellows_wayside_inn.htm (accessed March 17, 2014).

Kaplan, Susan. E-mail message to author. October 17, 2006.

———. Interview with author. Brunswick, Maine. May 15, 2014.

Longfellow, Henry Wadsworth. *The New England Tragedies.* Boston: Ticknor and Fields, 1868.

Longfellow's Wayside Inn. "Fun Facts." http://www.wayside.org/history/funfacts (accessed March 19, 2014).

Maine Historical Society Website. "Poems Database." http://www.hwlongfellow.org/poems_poem.php?pid=132.

McGraw Anderson, Patricia. *The Architecture of Bowdoin College.* Brunswick, ME: Bowdoin College Museum of Art, 1988.

Miller, Margot D. "Senior Speak." *Bowdoin Orient,* February 6, 2009.

"Mystery of 'Temple' Explosion Solved." *Bowdoin Alumnus,* 1926.

Nelsen, Mark. Interview by author. Brunswick, Maine. April 2, 2014.

New York Times. "John C. Donovan." October 5, 1984.

Norman, Michael, and Beth Scott. *Historic Haunted America.* New York: Tom Doherty Associates, LLC, 1996.

O'Brien, Rose. "Dead Ship of Harpswell." *Lewiston Journal,* October 29, 1955.

Osolin, Ned. Interview by author. Brunswick, Maine. April 2014.

Pitkin, David J. *Ghosts of the Northeast.* Salem, NY: Aurora Publications, 2002.

Roberts, Nancy. *Civil War Ghost Stories & Legends.* Columbia, SC: University of South Carolina Press, 1992.

Smith, Sam. "Down East Notes: The Ghost Ship of Harpswell." *Undernews,* September 10, 2012.

Smyth, George Adams. *Reminiscences of my Life.* Pasadena, CA: [s.n.], 1928.

Syphers, Dale. E-mail messages to author. April 2014.

Thomas A. Curtis obituary. *Brunswick (ME) Telegraph,* April 30, 1868.

Versluis, Arthur. "The 'Occult' in Nineteenth-Century America." In *The Occult in Nineteenth-Century America.* Edited by Cathy Gutierez. Aurora, CO: Davies Group, 2005.

Vincent, Staci. Interview by author. Brunswick, Maine. June 2011.

Whittemore, Joyce. Interview by author. Brunswick, Maine. April 30, 2014.

Whittier, John Greenleaf. "The Dead Ship of Harpswell." *Atlantic Monthly,* June 1866.

Wikipedia. "Alpheus Spring Packard, Sr." http://en.wikipedia.org/wiki/Alpheus_Spring_Packard,_Sr. (accessed April 12, 2014).

———. "Coffin (whaling family)." http://en.wikipedia.org/wiki/Coffin_(whaling_family) (accessed April 27, 2014).

———. "Fugitive Slave Act of 1850." http://en.wikipedia.org/wiki/Fugitive_Slave_Act_of_1850 (accessed March 12, 2014).

———. "Giles Corey" http://en.wikipedia.org/wiki/Giles_Corey (accessed May 2, 2014).

———. "Joshua Chamberlain." http://en.wikipedia.org/wiki/Joshua_Chamberlain (accessed May 1, 2014).

———. "Longfellow House." http://en.wikipedia.org/wiki/Longfellow_House (accessed March 17, 2014).

———. "William Hathorne." http://en.wikipedia.org/wiki/William_Hathorne (accessed May 1, 2014).

Zwicker, Roxie J. *Haunted Portland: From Pirates to Ghost Brides.* Charleston, SC: The History Press, 2007.

About the Author

David Francis has spent most of his career as a computer programmer. A native of Indiana, David earned a bachelor of arts in mathematics and English while studying at Indiana University. Upon graduating, he put both fields of study to use as an editorial specialist for the *Indiana University Mathematics Journal (IUMJ)*. After helping the *IUMJ* start its first venture into online publishing, David became more involved in technology and worked as a web coordinator at the University of Wyoming and then as a web developer for Salisbury University in Maryland. He joined Bowdoin College in 2001 and is now the senior interactive developer for the college's Digital and Social Media Department.

David developed an early appreciation for ghost stories when his older brothers and sisters began to host elaborate Halloween parties and adventures for the younger children in the family each year. Halloween is by far his favorite holiday, and preparations for that night begin months in advance in the Francis household.

David has always had a strong interest in history and a particular fascination for local history. Since living in Maine, he has enjoyed exploring the historical sites there, which are typically far less well known than other places in New England, even though they are frequently much older.

David and his wife, Rebecca, live in Brunswick, Maine, with their one dog and six cats.